Timber in Playgrounds

Edgar Stubbersfield

and

Ralph Bailey

Copyright © 2021 Edgar Stubbersfield and Ralph Bailey

All rights reserved.

ISBN: 978-0-6486781-4-4

CONTENTS

Introduction 3

Scope of this Guide 4

1 standards and fitness for purpose 5

Introduction 5

What is Sapwood, Heartwood and Heart? 7

Preservative Treatment in Playgrounds. 9

What is Lyctus? 12

Considerations When Choosing a Timber Species 13

    Availability 14

    Fire 14

    Termite Resistance. 15

    What do the Durability Ratings Mean? 15

    In-ground Durability Class 1 and 2 16

    Above-ground Durability Class 1 and 2 Timber. 18

    Interlocking Grain 19

    Shrinkage 19

    Greasy to the Touch 20

    Royal Species 20

Antibacterial Properties 22

Use Standard Trade Names Only. 22

    Why it is important to use the correct name. 23

Imported Hardwood 23

    Kwila (Merbau) 24

    Larch 24

    Robinia 25

    Meranti 27

    Rubberwood 28

Conclusion 36

2 Sawn timber in playgrounds 37

Introduction 37

What About Kiln Dried Timber? 38

What About Recycled Timber? 38

Considerations When Specifying Sawn Timber 39

    Heart 40

    Heartwood 42

    Sapwood 43

  Natural feature 43
  Cypress 46
  Pine 47
  General 47
 Surface Finish 48
 Independent Verification of Grade 49

3 Round Timber in playgrounds 50
 Introduction 50
 Splitting Heads 51
  Splitting on low shrinkage species (Maximum 3%) 52
  Splitting on higher shrinkage species (3.1 to 7.5%) 52
 Longitudinal Checks 54
 Preparing Round Timber 55
 Fastening. 56
 Critical Zone 56
 Seats and Steppers 57

4 SPECIAL CONSIDERATIONS WITH CCA 58
 How Dangerous is CCA? 58
 What Can be Done with Existing CCA Infrastructure? 61
 Avoiding CCA in design and specification 62

5 timber specifications 63
 Considerations When Specifying Playground Timber 63
 Hardwood-Sawn 63
  Hardwood sawn-above-ground 63
  Hardwood sawn - in-ground 64
  Hardwood kiln dried decking 64
  Hardwood Unseasoned decking 65
 Cypress Sawn 65
  Cypress-sawn all applications except decking 66
  Cypress-sawn decking 66
 Plantation Pine Sawn 66
  Pine - General 66
  Plantation pine - above-ground - sawn 66
  Plantation pine - above-ground – decking 66
  Plantation pine - In-ground – Sawn, self-supporting 66
  Plantation pine - In-ground – sawn free standing 67
 Hardwood Natural Rounds 67
  Hardwood, natural round - In-ground – self supporting 67

    Hardwood, natural round - In-ground - free standing 68

Cypress Natural Rounds 68
    Cypress natural round - In-ground self-supporting 68
    Cypress natural round - In-ground free standing 69

Pine Natural Rounds 69
    Pine – natural round – above-ground 69
    Pine – natural round – in-ground self-supporting 69
    Pine – natural round – in-ground free standing 70

6 Engaging with the ground 71

introduction 71

Embedded Posts 71

The Importance of Site Location 72

Embedded Timber Sizes 73

Embedding Posts in the Ground 74

Pole Bandage and Rods 75

Method of Installation of the Post 76

Embedment Depth 76

Posts in Supports 77
    Blade type supports 80
    Log seats and steppers 83
    Is galvanising even necessary? 83
    Paint – general 84

Terminating timber paths 85

7 fasteners 87

General Considerations 87

Fastener Material Type 88

Vandal Resistance 90

Some Observations Regarding Fasteners 92
    Coachscrews 92
    Self-drilling Type 17 screws 93
    Barrel Nuts 93
    Brad hole T nut 94
    Nail Plates 95
    Custom fasteners. 95

8 Construction details 96

Decking 96
    Fastening from underneath 96
    Face Fixing 96

Changes of direction	98
Edge Treatment	*98*
Mitre joints	*98*
End sealing	*99*
End and Edge Clearances	*99*
Connecting Timber	*101*
Identify Critical Areas	*102*
Attaching Accessories	*102*
Inspection of Fasteners	*104*

9 Documentation and certification 105

General	*105*
Minimum Documentation	*105*
Before you Start	*106*
The Responsibilities of the Parties	*106*
Equipment designer	106
Playground designer	106
Equipment Supplier	106
Playground installer	107
Surfacing manufacturer/supplier	107
Surfacing installer	107
Playground Certifier	107
International Certification	*108*
Equipment Without Current Certification	*108*

10 Inspection and Maintenance 109

Frequency of Inspection	*109*
Inspection of Timber Playgrounds	*111*
General and tools required	111
Areas to Inspect	*111*
Species	111
Decay at groundline	112
Termite attack	112
Sharp points	113
Finger entrapment associated with splits	113
Splinters	114
Longitudinal splits	114
Fasteners	115
Maintenance and Surface Finishes	*115*
Preservatives	115
Finishes, general	116

    Leaching of Tannins 116
    Paint... 117
    Clear coatings 120
    Penetrating Oils 122
    Lanolin Based Oils 123
    Painting Steel Supports - general 124
    Decorative finishes 124
    Corrosion Resistant Finishes 124

11 Case Histories 125

    Playground on the Broadwater, Southport, Queensland... 125

    Arab Dhow in Qatar 127

    Queen's Park, Ipswich 129

    Ports North, Cairns 131

Appendix 1. observations on post supports 134

Check List 136

Source of Images 145

Works Cited 147

ABOUT THE AUTHORS 151

ACKNOWLEDGMENTS

Both Ted and Ralph wish to acknowledge the pioneering leadership provided to the Queensland timber industry, indeed the whole Australian industry through a very remarkable organisation, the Timber Research and Development Advisory Council (Qld) better known as TRADAC. This organisation and the people who worked tirelessly to advance best practice in timber use are remembered with much respect by all who used their guides and services. A special acknowledgement goes to Colin Mackenzie who joined the organisation as Technical Director in the mid 1970's and served with it till it was merged with Timber Queensland in about 2003 where he continued till his retirement. On "retirement" he is still giving excellent support to the industry.

We have both worked closely with these organisations to support their work and have given papers at their training events where our specialised expertise has been sought out.

INTRODUCTION

Interest in playground design has been heightened in recent years as the recognition of the importance of nature play to children has been acknowledged and timber use is considered an essential part of nature play. There is recognition that challenge and discovery are necessary design features in children's playgrounds and a recognised need to incorporate natural experiences, textures and colours that increase sensory experiences – the five senses, touch, taste, sight, hearing and smell are all well-known but there are others which include vestibular (the sense of balance) and proprioception (knowing which parts of your body are where without looking).

Timber in playground design, along with rocks, soil (mud), sand, water, mulch, living plants help provide these sensory opportunities. Utilising timber in playground designs (and through this book we will illustrate some different possibilities) as well as living trees with trunks and branches to climb or swing on or from are the tools of the playground designer. It is vital to understand timber types for strength and durability and know how to use timber, to join it and to finish it. This book explores what has been done, what has been successful and what has not been successful in the use of timber in playgrounds and we believe that this will enable designers to make better design decisions in future playground designs.

This guide is intended to enable designers to understand what successful use of timber in playgrounds entails. This guide will explain the limitations of the Australian Standards and then lead designers through the choices that are necessary to specify timber in a way that is not just Code compliant but more importantly, fit for purpose. Subsequent chapters will give guidance on how to use that timber by discussing appropriate fasteners, fixings and timber joints. The book will also examine and discuss several case histories.

Ralph Bailey

SCOPE OF THIS GUIDE

Edgar (Ted) Stubbersfield is arguably Australia's leading authority on detailing weather exposed timber while Ralph Bailey is a respected architect and the designer of outstanding playgrounds who has a lifetime of experience with timber. This book combines the expertise of these two authors and applies their considerable skills to documenting best practice in the use of timber in playgrounds. The scope of this book is intentionally limited simply to best practice when using timber in playgrounds. This book will provide playground designers, builders, inspectors, and clients the following

- An understanding of how Australian climatic conditions need an Australian answer to durability of timber
- An understanding of how to choose an appropriate timber for a particular application
- An understanding of the importance of preservation of timber
- How to specify appropriate grades of timber for round and sawn hardwood, cypress and plantation pine
- How to engage with the ground in ways that require minimal maintenance
- How to detail timber joints in a playground for durability, and
- How to choose fasteners that are fit for purpose

To complete this guide, as well as the case histories that illustrate what is presented, there is a design checklist which highlights the critical points we describe. In this way a designer, manufacturer, supplier, or provider can ensure he/she has attended to all the critical details that will impact upon a long-life playground with minimal maintenance.

What this book does not provide, nor is intended to provide is a ready reference for the many common elements from the Australian Standards that make up a safe playground. Such a reference already exists, *A guide to the Australian Playground Standards* by Andrew Reedy. This guide can be obtained by contacting Andrew on info@playcheck.com.au.

Disclaimer
The information shown herein, does not constitute a complete design nor cover every application that may be encountered. It is intended as an aid to, not a substitute for suitably qualified professional architects, landscape architects, engineers and playground inspectors and certifiers.

Figure 1. Our understanding of playground safety has changed over the years.

1 STANDARDS AND FITNESS FOR PURPOSE

Introduction

Understanding playground standards, and other relevant standards of supply and construction etc. is a vital part of the playground designer's toolkit. But equally important is to understand their limitations. Directions for the use of timber in playgrounds are given in the Australian variations for *AS4685.1-2021, Playground equipment and surfacing, Part 0 Playground equipment and surfacing Development, installation, inspection, maintenance and operation and Part 1: General safety requirements and test methods*. So what value are these guidelines for a playground designer who follows them? This story will explain the importance of this question. Many years ago, a client came to Ted's sawmill in South East Queensland with a set of plans for a new house and sought prices for timber to the nominated grades and sizes on the plans. The exposed Oregon rafters were a single length that extended from the apex of the roof and over the verandah. The builder was from Victoria which explained why his practices were different from those used in Queensland locality. Ted told him that, locally, builders would use hardwood for such an application, but the client replied that he had been a builder for 25 years and that he knew what he was doing and if he did not want to sell Oregon to him, he would go to someone who would. So, Ted dutifully did the take off and quoted according to the Australian Standard grade nominated. Ted's price was accepted and he then ordered the material to that grade and then shipped them to site.

About six months later, everything went horribly wrong from the owner's perspective. Knots started to fall out and, generally, it was not looking as good as it did when it was first installed. Ted's customer received legal aid and sued Ted for $50,000 to take off his roof and the Oregon ceiling lining and beams and replace them. As some of the timber was not to the grade specified Ted, in turn, sued the supplier. The first thing the judge said was, "Australian Standards do not have the force of law; I am only interested in whether the timber was fit for purpose." Then followed two days of evidence and one of legal argument with three barristers and solicitors in attendance. The costs were horrendous with stress to match. Fortunately, he was not dealing with a personal injury. Ted's client won just over $100 in damages, so he had to pay the builder's expenses. Legal argument came down to a case of bicycle bells sold in the 1800's! Ted was faced with a dilemma; on one side there was clear but legally useless guidance in an Australian Standard and on the other an unfathomable minefield of obscure legal precedents. His solution was to only give lip service to the Standards but to concentrate on products that, in his judgement, were fit for purpose.

Fortunately, in the course of time, the Building Code of Australia (BCA) now the National Construction Code (NCC) incorporated a limited number of Australian Standards as primary documents, such as *AS1684.2 Residential timber framed construction - Non-cyclonic areas*, *AS1720.1 Timber structures - Design methods* and *AS1720.5 Timber Structures – Timber properties* as primary references in that Code[1] Other commonly used Standards in the timber industry such as *AS1604.1 Specification for preservative treatment Sawn and round timber* and the grading standards AS2082 *Timber—Hardwood—Visually stress-graded for structural purposes* and AS2858 *Timber - Softwood - Visually stress-graded for structural purposes* are secondary references that get applied and given the force of law through being referenced in the primary standard. Further, the BCA and then the NCC in its Queensland regulations

---
[1] Found in Section B1.4 of Volume 1 of the 2019 edition.

incorporated a State Government publication, *Construction Timbers in Queensland* (CTIQ) which gave a legal, "deemed to comply" basis for designing for a 15 and a 50-year design life with timber in Class 1 and Class 10 structures.[2] **Unfortunately for the playground designer, and all those associated with playgrounds there is no such clear legal underpinning for the timber guidelines in AS4685.1 parts 0 and 1.**[3]

General guidance for the use of timber in playgrounds is given in the Australian Variations to the European standard *EN 1176-1:2017 Playground equipment and surfacing - Part 1: General safety requirements and test methods*. It is issued here as *AS 4685.1:2021 Playground equipment and surfacing, Part 1: General safety requirements and test methods*. Standards Australia understandably wanted a straight adoption of the EN standard, but the playground committee members were able to make a compelling case for the Australian variation (Appendix ZZ) as local Australian conditions are different from Europe's. These differences include:

- The UV is about 40% higher than at the same latitude in the northern hemisphere
- The climate is generally much harsher
- The agents of attack are different e.g., termites, fungi, and
- The Australian timbers available are different and can be far more durable.

There are two standards mentioned the variations[4] which are:

- *AS 1604.1 Specification for preservative treatment, Part 1: Sawn and round timber*[5]; and,
- *AS 5604 Timber – Natural durability ratings*.

Though not specifically mentioned by name in the playground equipment standard, other standards that refer to the structural properties of the timber will frequently be mentioned by designers either directly or incidentally through references such as F14 and F17 and MGP12. These standards are:

- *AS 2082 Timber—Hardwood—Visually stressgraded for structural purposes*
- *AS 2858 Timber—Softwood—Visually stressgraded for structural purposes*; and,
- *AS 3519 Timber – Machine proof grading*

As it is common for playgrounds to have some decking, the standards that apply for kiln dried decking are:

---

[2] Department of Agriculture and Fisheries. *Construction Timbers in Queensland. Book 1: Definitions and Descriptions*. (Brisbane: Queensland Government. 2020) vii. It will be argued in the chapter on certification that playgrounds should probably be considered a Class 10B structure.

[3] We will later argue that playgrounds should probably be certified as a Class 10B structure, but the validity of this guideline could be contested.

[4] Clause 2.2

[5] AS 4685 only refers to the AS 1604 series. The other three which refer to plywood (Part 3), laminated veneer lumber (Part 4) and glued laminated lumber (Part 5) are not relevant to this book's discussion.

- *AS 2796.1 Timber—Hardwood—Sawn and milled products Part 1: Product specification*
- *AS 2796.2 Timber—Hardwood—Sawn and milled products Part 1: Grade description.*

It will be argued throughout this guide that strength-based specifications that were developed for items such as roof trusses and floor framing have little value in playgrounds. While structural issues are important, they must be accompanied by closer attention to detail such as durability and avoiding finger and foot entrapments, splintering, slip hazards etc. This results in a much higher specification than would be used ordinarily.

What is Sapwood, Heartwood and Heart?

Figure 2. End section of hardwood poles showing sapwood, heartwood and heart. A die has been added to distinguish the sapwood more clearly.

Figure 3. End section of pine log showing sapwood, heartwood and heart

Figure 4. End section of cypress logs showing sapwood, heartwood and heart. Note the small size of many stems

There are three terms which are basic for understanding and specifying and inspecting timber, these are *sapwood*, *heartwood*, also known as truewood and **heart**, also known as pith. Whilst the words "heartwood" and "wood with heart" sound very similar, they are different things and must be considered differently in playground design. The end sections of hardwood, pine and cypress are shown in Figure 2 to Figure 4 and each contain the three different areas of a tree that affect playground design:

- Sapwood, the live portion of the tree that transmits moisture and nutrients to the crown of the tree
- Heartwood, the dead central wood of the tree, and
- Heart, the centre of the tree which is made of juvenile wood.

Timber	Sapwood	True/Heartwood	Heart/pith
Hardwood	Not durable – can be treated	Sometimes durable – cannot be treated	Unstable – cannot be treated
Pine	Not durable – can be treated	Not durable – cannot be treated	Structural – not durable cannot be treated
Cypress	Not durable – cannot be treated with waterborne preservatives	Durable – cannot be treated	Structural – durable cannot be treated

Table 1.   The properties of the constituent parts of hardwood, pine, and cypress.

While hardwood, pine and cypress may have the three areas in common, the properties of each are quite different. The differences are summarised in Table 1. Should a designer have successfully delivered a playground made from cypress, the same design practices will not necessarily deliver the same results from hardwood or pine. The importance of these distinctions will be explained through this guide and be bought together in product and application specific specifications.

Preservative Treatment in Playgrounds.

Figure 5.　　A metal cap has done nothing to stop the untreated sapwood on this post from decaying

Figure 6.　　Rafters are housed into the untreated sapwood which is decaying

The playground standard anticipates that timber will be treated[6] and demands treatment if sapwood is more than 15% of the cross section for both inground and above-ground applications.[7] The only restriction is that CCA, a preservative using copper, chrome and arsenic, and creosote (derived from coal tar) are not to be used. It would be very unwise, from both a public safety perspective and through the high maintenance costs that must come as a consequence, to design and supply a playground using untreated timber. The exception is if it can be assured to be supplied (that is different to specified) in a durability Class 1 hardwood, and that the sapwood has been removed.

There are 73 different preservative codes listed in AS1604.1-2012[8] some (22) are discontinued, and some (8) are basically duplications. That still leaves a significant number of approved chemicals that, theoretically, can be encountered. As for the two preservatives excluded in the playground standard, it is highly unlikely you will ever encounter one that has creosote treatment, but we expect that there are many CCA units still in service simply because it worked so well.[9] The worldwide trend has been to change away from the highly effective and proven treatments such as CCA and move towards products that have sufficient toxicity but with less of a perceived health risk. Of those remaining approved preservatives there

---

[6] AS 4685.1:2021 4.1.3.2.

[7] AS 4685.1:2021 4.1.3.2 and 4.1.3.3.

[8] Table C1

[9] In nationwide controlled monitoring sites, CCA treated radiata proved to be the most effective preservative with all samples bar one still serviceable after 33 years and creosote was the next best. Cookson, L.J. *The In-ground Natural Durability of Australian Timbers*. (Melbourne: Forest and Wood Products Research and Development Corporation. 2004) 1.

is little concern[10] with them when used in playgrounds and there is no reason to go beyond the two excluded preservatives.

Hazard Level: Exposure & Biological Hazard AS1604.1-2012	Typical Use As quoted by AS 1604.1
H3 – Exterior above-ground subject to periodic wetting. Decay, termites, and borers	Weatherboards, fascia, window joinery, exterior framing and decking
H4 – Exterior in-ground. Subject to severe wetting. Decay, termites and borers	Fencing, greenhouses, pergolas and landscaping timbers
H5 – Exterior in-ground, with or in fresh water. Decay, termites and borers	Retaining walls, piling, house stumps, building poles, cooling tower fill
Table 2. Hazard levels relevant to playgrounds[11]	

The two hazard levels mentioned in the playground standard are H3 and H4 but, it will be argued, there is also a place for H5 or an equivalent. The treatment processes most likely to be encountered in Australian produced hardwood for H3 and which should only be used for H4 and H5 playground applications, are the waterborne Tanalith E, Micro Pro (both also known as copper azole) or alkaline copper quaternary known as ACQ. H5 can also be achieved with these chemicals but this is only done with CCA due to the high cost and low demand for the non-chrome, non-arsenic alternatives. Had the Standard been silent on CCA, that preservative is not permitted in playgrounds under the Australian Pesticides and Veterinary Medicines Authority (APVMA) guidelines for the approved use of this preservative. In pine, H3 can be achieved with light organic solvent preservatives (LOSP) which have the advantage of not wetting the timber and so there is no dimensional change and so no need to redry. LOSP preservatives are formulated to include both a fungicide and an insecticide. Applications beyond H3 can only be met with waterborne preservatives. Many consider that H3 LOSP is not as robust as the waterborne preservatives.

NOTE: When using waterborne preservatives with pine a water repellent, usually a wax, should be specified.[12]

---

[10] Enquiries were made with Lonza and Koppers Performance Chemicals and Lonza.
[11] AS 1604.1-2012 Table 1.1
[12] Such a product is available as an addition to Tanalith E manufactured by Arch Wood Protection.

Figure 7. Complete failure of "treated" pine in Sydney after 12 years

Figure 8. Incised pine

As mentioned in Table 1, cypress sapwood cannot be treated successfully with waterborne preservatives, but the sizes frequently used are cut with the heart in the centre and contain little or no sapwood so, in these cases, it is not relevant in any discussion of treatment of cypress playground timber. The heart and heartwood are naturally exceptionally durable. Pine, on the other hand is not durable and while the sapwood is treatable, the heartwood and heart are not easily penetrated by preservative. If timber containing significant amounts of heart e.g., 100x100 or larger, are put through the treatment process it does not result in "treated" timber, simply timber that is "coloured" on the outside. The consequence is shown in the H3 applications in Figure 7. The images were taken after 12 years but the members had been unsound for some time beforehand. Imagine the potential repercussions from a swing made with this type of material. At the time of writing there is no national accreditation scheme for timber preservation, and, in its absence, a designer should proceed with caution when durability is only ensured through chemical means.[13]

Incised pine, which is common overseas but not in Australia, in Ted's opinion is a way of ensuring correct penetration has been achieved. Timber is "Incised: when it is run through a set of toothed rollers which forms small slits in the surface that fill with preservative (Figure 8). Though incised pine does not have

---

[13] The records required for due diligence with treated pine is discussed in Ted's *Timber Preservation Guide*.

the smooth appearance of normal dressed pine, it has the advantage of having reduced splitting.[14] As the time of writing, there are few incisors in the country and none of these are producing structural timber. If a H4 or H5 application in pine is considered, it should be understood that it will not be available as an off the shelf product, but if the quantity is large enough it can be manufactured on demand but at high cost.[15] The supply of sawn pine for posts should be considered impractical if not impossible. The designer should therefore defer to the superior performance of cypress and the best hardwoods.

As for hardwoods, there is no requirement under AS1604 for the sapwood of durability Class 1 and 2 timber to be treated if it only makes up 15% of the cross-section area. Despite that, Ted's recommendation would be to treat all sapwood. While 15% is not a great deal and structural timber is allowed 20% of the cross section to be untreated sapwood, there are two issues related to playgrounds that treatment will resolve. Untreated sapwood is classed as durability Class 4 both above and below ground. It will decay as shown in Figure 9 when exposed to the weather and this could lead to finger entrapments and trip hazards.[16] As well, sapwood in structural timber must be treated if it is lyctus susceptible, and some of the best timbers for playgrounds are lyctus susceptible.

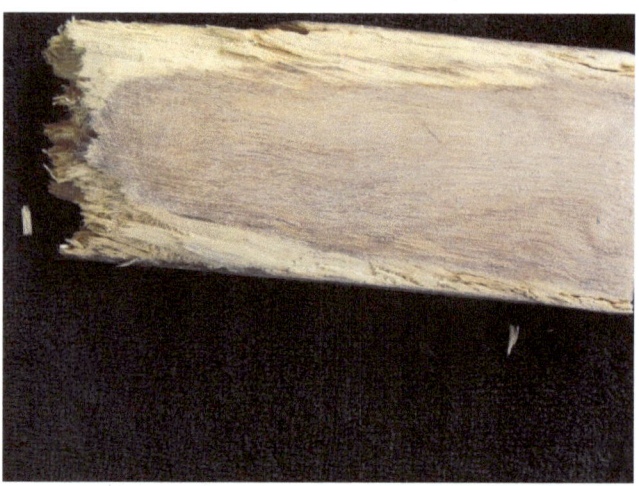

Figure 9.   Decay at end of beam in untreated blackbutt sapwood

What is Lyctus?
The potential for decay in weather exposed untreated sapwood is well understood but less well understood is lyctus attack. The lyctus beetle sometimes called the powder post beetle for good reason, lays its eggs in the sapwood and its larvae (Figure 12) will eat the sapwood and literally turn it to powder. This will occur more quickly than decay and will have a very un-settling effect on the asset owner. Even a small edge subject to Lyctus attack will be very noticeable. Lyctus attack is generally not an issue in Victoria and Tasmania.

For playground applications such as decking, the stabilisation of the sapwood is important because, if it decays, trip hazards and with framing members vees develop so finger entrapment may occur. The lighter domestic style decking may, in places, be virtually all sapwood, so treatment is critical. Lyctus attack of the sapwood will occur well before the decay of untreated sapwood and will occur whether the timber is protected or not. Had the piece of blackbutt in Figure 9 been used internally as an exposed ceiling beam, and even with a higher proportion of sapwood, it would have exhibited no degrade of the sapwood as lyctus does not attack this species and so does not require any treating when used internally (unlike the

---

[14] This is discussed in Philip D. Evans, *The effects of incising on the checking of wood: A review*, International Wood Products Journal, 7:1 (2016),12-25,

[15] Hong Teck Lee. Pers. Com. November 3, 2020

[16] This happens through vees developing at joints and the deck surface not being flat.

spotted gum in Figure 10 and Figure 11).

Figure 10. Lyctus attack in roof truss

Figure 11. Lyctus attack in roof member

Figure 12. Lyctus larvae.

The situation with Lyctus susceptible timbers such as spotted gum and tallowwood is quite different. These timbers have higher levels of starch in the sapwood.

We have found that there is an expectation that timber can be supplied without sapwood. Ted's observation of the ex. 38 and 50 mm decking he produced is that perhaps one piece in three contains significant amounts of sapwood. To supply sapwood free timber, in effect, means that much of a very limited resource (timber) is wasted and this is poor stewardship. Very few of any ex. 75mm members would be totally free of sapwood.

Considerations When Choosing a Timber Species

When timber is in contact with the ground, AS4685.1-2021 requires that the timber be an inground durability Class 1 or 2 to *AS 5604 Timber – Natural durability ratings* with untreated sapwood not exceeding 15% or alternatively, the timber is to be treated to H4. For above-ground applications the requirements are the same except that the treatment need only be H3. That specification is extremely broad and for timbers with natural durability, that gives 93 species available for in-ground use and 99 for above-ground.[17] The reality is that only a handful of the close to 100 permitted species are fit for purpose when it comes to playground construction. What follows is a discussion of timber properties that are relevant to playground design and construction. This is summarised in Table 7 where the authors' recommendations for species are highlighted.

---

[17] Table A1.

Availability

Availability of timber has two considerations:

- How much of the timber is actually available; and,
- Does the distance to site warrant specifying a certain species?

Fortunately, a playground usually does not require a large amount of timber so there is a greater chance of obtaining a less common species than had you been requiring the many cubic metres that may be needed to build say, a boardwalk or bridge. But a playground designer should make themselves acquainted with what is readily available. In Queensland say, spotted gum is readily available at about 69% of the state forest cut but Gympie messmate is only about 1.25%. Both will work well in an above-ground application and despite Gympie Messmate's low percentage it should be available in the quantities needed. Other species drawn from the 100 or so permitted may be much less available. But what is not readily available from the local timber merchant does not mean that it is not readily available from a specialty supplier such as those supplying brigalow and lancewood natural rounds. The New South Wales forest mix is different from Queensland and different again from Victoria and Western Australia. All this means that you cannot just pick a species from a list but must do research for your own market.

Again, the species that are common in Western Australia can be less durable, and even far less durable than the best available on the east coast. It would make little sense to bring jarrah across the continent from Western Australia, but the case can be made for taking spotted gum or Gympie messmate across to Perth.

Fire

Perhaps what is seen as a major shortcoming of timber is the apparent rather obvious observation that it burns, but is it a truism? *AS 3959-2009 Construction of buildings in bushfire-prone areas* lists seven species that can be used in bushfire prone areas without the need for additional fire retardants. These are blackbutt, kwila (merbau), red ironbark,[18] river red gum, silvertop ash, spotted gum and turpentine. If vandalism of a playground or decking by fire is considered a possibility a bushfire resistant species with the other necessary properties should be used. Pine or white cypress are not an option where natural fire resistance is required.

---

[18] This is a different species to narrow-leaved and broad-leaved red ironbark which are not bushfire resistant. Red ironbark is sometimes known as mugga.

Figure 13.   If vandalism by fire is likely, choose a bushfire resistant timber

Termite Resistance.

Not every species is readily eaten by termites and the list of those that are resistant is found in AS5604.[19] That is not to say that they are never eaten by termites but rather that they are "resistant". That species will be the last thing on their menu and termites will only turn to it when other sources of food are exhausted. Resistance refers to the heartwood and not the untreated sapwood which is never durable and can be eaten by termites if not treated. Termite resistance of selected species is given in Table 7. The heart of resistant species, while still classed as resistant may be less resistant than the heartwood (refer to Figure 2, Figure 3 and Figure 4) for the illustration of these terms).

What do the Durability Ratings Mean?

A list of expected design life ranges is given in AS 5604 (Table 3) but there are many variables that affect the actual result. The expectancy must be given as a range as many things affect the actual outcome, including:

- Whether the timber is preservative treated
- The manufacturing process, e.g., dressed timber in the weather can have a shorter life
- Whether best practice in detailing was followed, e.g., are surfaces moisture shedding
- Whether the timber is painted or regularly oiled

---

[19] Should the reader not have a copy of AS 5604, the same information can be found in *CTIQ* which is a free Queensland State Government publication what has the force of law in NCC matters. It is also available in Bootle's Wood in Australia which every design office should have in its library.

- The climatic conditions, and
- The size and orientation of the timber, e.g., decking may have a shorter life expectancy than joists.

Durability class	Above-ground life expectancy	In-ground life expectancy
1	> 40 years	> 25 years
2	15 to 40 Years	15 to 25 years
3	7 to 15 years	5 to 15 years
4	0 to 7 years	0 to 5 years

Table 3. Natural durability rating to AS 5604-2005

The ratings in Table 3 above have been determined by taking test specimens of sound untreated heartwood, (35x35 mm for above-ground applications and 50x50 mm for in-ground) and installing them in a number of locations around Australia. These are then monitored for many years. While it is unlikely any application is going to have a smaller size than those monitored, a larger member size will result in a longer service life. By suitably increasing the size a service life of 50 years, even in the tropics can be achieved.[20] The importance of this point is elaborated upon in the chapter, *Engaging with the Ground*.

In-ground Durability Class 1 and 2

Ted has observed that the distinction between in-ground and above-ground applications has not always been understood and observed in specifying. *AS5604-2003 Timber – Natural durability ratings (revised in 2005)* replaced an earlier standard that only listed in-ground durability. A replacement was necessary as the agents of attack for in-ground use were different from those above-ground. Take spotted gum for instance. It was classed as a durability Class 2 timber, and in-ground it was not as durable as ironbark but in above-ground situations where failures could be life threatening, such as a crossarm on a powerpole, it excelled. So frequently, designers would ask for durability Class 1 timber for above-ground applications and so exclude a readily available and successful timber or ask for durability Class 1 and 2 which permitted spotted gum but also permitted lower performing species. AS 5604 very wisely separates the two applications.

Figure 14. 125x125 durability Class 1 posts directly embedded in ground are still sound after 25 years in Brisbane (though not a recommended application to Ralph's mind)

---

[20] CTIQ, Vol 1 (Revised 2020), 24.

AS4685.1-2021 permits the use of In-ground durability Class 1 and 2 timbers for applications in-ground contact.[21] Caution needs to be exercised with this recommendation.

Species	In-ground durability	Location and total duration of trial				
		Brisbane 36 years	Innisfail 36 years	Sydney 35.3 years	Walpeup 35.7 years	Melbourne 33.4 years
E. pilularis (blackbutt)	2	5.2	3.2	13.6	23.9	23.9
C. maculate & C. citrodora (spotted gum)	2	8.5	8.5	15.0	18.1	>33.4
E. cloeziana (Gympie messmate)	1	23.9	13.8	25	>37.5	>33.4
E. microcorys (Tallowwood)	1	27.6	23.9	32.6	>37.5	>33.4
E. paniculate (Gray ironbark)	1	26.3	26.3	>35.3	26.9	>33.4
E. sideroxylon (Red ironbark)	1	22.8	26.3	25.5	27.6	>33.4

Table 4.   Median inground durability of 50x50 hardwood achieved at five trial sites.[22]

The wide variability of in-ground durability Class 1 and 2 timbers in field trials around Australia show that a durability Class 2 timber could have a short life indeed. These timbers could well fail in the expected service life of a playground in the tropics yet perform adequately in Melbourne. Conversely, a playground that was a success in Cairns can be successfully transplanted in Melbourne. Ted's recommendation is to learn the best practices of design that are needed for the tropics and use them everywhere.

Figure 15.   Free standing playground items need the highest durability and attention to detail for installation.

Ted has a particular concern with the use of durability Class 2 in-ground timbers in free standing applications, i.e., two post structures (Figure 15). A friend's brother was killed when a similar structure rotted at ground line and collapsed, crushing his skull. Some of these swings using 200x200 hardwood start at 500 kg and can approach one tonne depending on the model. In-ground timber is also very susceptible to decay if it is installed incorrectly. Correct installation is discussed in the Chapter, *Engaging with the ground*.

---

[21] Standards Australia. *AS 5604-2005 Timber—Natural durability ratings*. (Sydney: Standards Australia International Ltd, 2005) 3.1.3.1.
[22] Cookson. *Natural …*, 4&5.

Above-ground Durability Class 1 and 2 Timber.

AS4685.1-2021 permits the use of above-ground durability Class 1 and 2 timbers for applications that are not in-ground contact.[23] Caution needs to be exercised with this recommendation also. With the introduction of *AS5604 Timber – Natural durability ratings* and the addition of an extra column for above-ground use, basically, the ratings for inground use, with some exceptions were moved up one grade. This meant that a durability Class 3 in-ground timber, e.g., rose gum, now became an above-ground 2. The problem is that an in-ground 3 was never considered suitable for external use. A warning was issued by Timber Queensland about specifying and using above-ground 2 timbers externally and this was incorporated into Ted's guide *The Seven Deadly Sins of External Timber Design*.as Sin Number 7. The comparison in Table 5 is from this book.

Species	Heartwood - In-ground Durability Class	Heartwood - Above-ground Durability Class
Ash, silvertop	3	2
Blackbutt	2	1
Gum, blue, Sydney	3	2
Gum rose	3	2
Gum, spotted	2	1
Ironbark	1	1
Jarrah	2	2
Kapur	3	2
Kwila/Merbau	3	1
Stringybark, brown	3	2
Table 5.	In-ground and above-ground durability comparisons as per AS 5604-2005.	

Considering this, Ted would strongly advise against using above-ground durability Class 2 timbers for playgrounds and only use durability Class 1. That still leaves 68 possibilities under AS5604-2005 but, only a handful of these are truly fit for playground construction. This are identified and discussed further in this chapter under *Royal Species*.

---

[23] 3.1.3.1.

Interlocking Grain

Figure 16.   Straight grained turpentine

Figure 17.   Interlocked grain Gympie messmate

Obviously, timber can splinter, and this is a major concern to asset owners. Not all timber is equally prone to splintering and those where the grain runs in a single direction are more likely to do it. A grain is called interlocked when it spirals around the axis of the tree but reverses its direction for periods of years. This results in alternating directions of the spiral grain. Those timbers that have interlocking grain have less of a propensity to produce larger splinters. If splinters are of concern, the designer should use a species that has or often has interlocking grain. The nature of the grain of selected species is listed in Table 7.

Shrinkage

As timber loses its moisture it shrinks. This is unavoidable and generally it is not a serious issue and we have been able to accommodate the shrinkage characteristics of our unique timbers for over 200 years or at least we used to be able to! Ted has seen an increased used of the term 'KD" the abbreviation for "kiln dried" and has observed that it is almost used as a throwaway line with little consideration of whether it is necessary and whether it is even possible to achieve. That is without any consideration of the added costs and possibly three months minimum extra lead time. But above all that, the bigger question is whether you should kiln dry. If you only put enough water in the kettle to make a single cup of coffee as your part in saving the planet, why would you put 17 megajoules or so into a cubic metre of hardwood, with the associated costs and delay, if it is not necessary and the sun will dry it for free?

There are some basic considerations:
- It is not possible to commercially dry beyond 50-55 mm thick
- Large cross section re-sawn recycled sizes are not dry and behave like freshly cut timber
- KD timber will absorb moisture and expand in the weather, and
- Commercially available KD framing timber may not be suitable for playgrounds

Pine, for all intents and purposes is only available kiln dried and in sizes up to 45 mm thick while cypress has a low shrinkage rate of only 2.6-3%[24] so a designer would not normally consider having that product

---

[24] Sources vary, Keith Bootle gives it as about 3.0% (Wood ..., 270) and the Department of Primary Industries, Forest Service gave it as 2.6% (*Timber Species Note 28*, no publication data). The higher figure will be used hereafter for simplicity.

kiln dried unless it is only 25 mm thick. The designer need only consider shrinkage when designing with hardwood though now it does have a limited but increasing availability as kiln dried, but in a limited range of species and sizes. As was mentioned, it is not commercially possible to dry timber beyond 50-55 mm thick which means that items such as 100x100 mm posts (or larger) and 75 mm wide members as may be found in playgrounds simply cannot be supplied kiln dried. Providing lower shrinkage timbers (up to 6% tangential) are used, it is possible to design to accommodate shrinkage. Some less common hardwood species can have shrinkage as low as 1.5% tangential but can be as high as 13%.

Sometimes, however, there are more refined items such as the Arab dhow featured in the *Case Histories*, where the beauty of the timber is intended to be capitalised upon rather than just functional matters. In these situations, the timber should be kiln dried. Unlike flooring where the moisture content is critical, there is considerable leeway with the moisture in timber used for external furniture when it is considered that it could be in the rain for a week. The requirement for light decking is between 18 and 10 percent[25] and for furniture is between 13 and 8 percent.[26] Weather exposed playgrounds will have requirements more in keeping with light decking, but the timber industry has long recognised that 18% is too high, and We suggest a maximum of 15%.[27] However, it should be pointed out that the standards for general house framing are lower than that required for playgrounds, especially prestige pieces.

Movement must be expected even with kiln dried timber given the wide range of Equilibrium Moisture Contents that can be experienced in the different parts of Australia as well as about a 3% change in the one locality over a year. A less well-known measurement of shrinkage is "Unit Shrinkage" which is the dimension change for each percent change in moisture and for spotted gum that is 0.38%. This means that a 150 mm kiln dried piece still changes in dimension by 1.7 mm over the year. The designer should still design to accommodate shrinkage particularly when considering the gap between boards.

Greasy to the Touch

Two timbers that are especially durable, spotted gum and tallowwood are described as "greasy to the touch". These two can have exceptional durability but it is uncertain what effect this characteristic has.

Royal Species

With close on 100 species of eligible hardwood to choose from in AS 5604, how does the uninitiated know what are the very best species to use?

A study of the natural durability of 77 Australian timbers[28] identified the ten most durable species for in-ground applications.[29] The most durable, raspberry jam (*Acacia acuminata*) is a shrub from Western Australia meaning natural rounds over 2.0 m in length are virtually unobtainable. Others have such little

---

[25] AS 2796.1-1999, 4.2
[26] AS 2796.3-1999 2.1
[27] At 18% the timber has only done half its shrinkage and 15% was the upper limit under the now repealed Timber Users Marketing Act in Queensland.
[28] There are probably over 200 species milled commercially in Australia.
[29] Cookson. *Natural …*, 1.

availability that they do not register on the harvesting statistics for Queensland and New South Wales or represent figures so low that they need to be ignored for all practical purposes. So how does a specifier know what species to use? When Ted and Ralph were young, there was a simple term that was commonly used when durable timber was required. It would be ordered as "royal species". This has been defined as "A collection of eucalypt timbers which command a premium in price because of their great durability and strength".[30] But what constitutes this collection? Ted has met people who claim to have a seen a definitive list, but no one has been able to point him to a document where it can actually be found.[31] Until such a list can be found, the prevailing and probably correct view is that this was a marketing term adopted by the industry. An old (90 years plus) senior forester recalled it this way - to be a royal species the timber had to be:

- Highly durable
- Readily available
- Extractable, and
- Have a ready market.

The significance of the last three points is that the timber was not a "boutique" or "craft" species that is not available in large enough quantities to be commercial. For structural timber, royal species included grey and the red ironbark, spotted gum (above-ground applications), tallowwood and yellow stringybark to which Ted would add Gympie messmate. The list varied from state to state and in Western Australia included jarrah and karri despite being of lower durability than the eastern Australian list.[32]

Unfortunately, on searching for this term on the internet, Ted found some mills in New South Wales advertising very inappropriate species as being "royal". So, a very useful description has been devalued and effectively lost. You cannot go wrong with the old forester's list as far as durability is concerned. You can go wrong when you then insist on a species that has low availability.[33] You can go wrong also when you choose a species on colour and not on durability. Ted's preference for above-ground applications would be for spotted gum because of its ready availability and natural oils. Notwithstanding confusion over the term, we will still use the "royal species" term through this book.

---

[30] Timber Secretarial Group. *Dictionary of Timber Terms* (Timber Secretarial Group: Sydney U.D.) 12.

[31] The closest Ted has come to a list is found in the Road and Traffic Authority report *Timber truss road bridges* - A strategic approach to conservation, July 2011 where it says on Page 16 "These bridges need 'royal' species (Grey Box, Ironbark, Tallowwood and Grey Gum) as used in the original designs. Lesser timbers such as Blackbutt or Spotted Gum are inferior, have less strength and deteriorate at a faster rate, thus requiring more frequent replacement". (New South Wales Government, July 2011). The report can be found at http://www.rms.nsw.gov.au/documents/projects/key-build-programs/maintenance/timber-truss-road-bridges/timber-truss-road-bridges-report-july11.pdf. Spotted gum would be a sought-out species for bridge work in Queensland but this may well reflect the variability between fast and slow grown timber.

[32] Smith, Walter. *Pers. Com.* Jan 18, 2013.

[33] A few years ago, Ted quoted a large quantity of tallowwood architectural battens. This species makes up less than 1% of the Queensland forestry harvest but it is more common in NSW. We found one NSW mill that may have been able to supply at the future time required and another that could guarantee supply. There was 20% difference in price between definite and maybe. If costed on a possibility it may have caused major problems at the time of supply.

Antibacterial Properties

The antibacterial properties of eucalyptus and melaleuca oil are well known. What seems to be unexplored is the antibacterial properties of the timber itself. When Ted was sawmilling he supplied a large quantity of ironbark piggery slats which surprised him as concrete and steel were much easier to purchase and install. His brother-in-law, a consultant in the piggery industry advised him that, counter intuitively, the bacteria load was lower on timber than on the alternatives. In 2020, a friend in Japan, Aki San of Kurata Co approached him asking for information about what happens to bacteria on Australian eucalypts. Unfortunately, Ted had no reference he could quote so she simply had it tested at the Shizuoka Industrial Research Institute for Testing. There under the guidance of their specialists, they tested the resistance of *Staphylococcus aureus* and *E. coli* when in contact with spotted gum.

Figure 18. Antibacterial certification of spotted gum in Japan.

The results were that these organisms disappeared after 24 hours! Kurata Co now sell spotted gum with their own logo (Figure 18) espousing its antimicrobial properties. Note that the text JIS Z 2801 below the logo relates to the test method which is designed to quantitatively test the ability of hard surfaces to inhibit the growth of microorganisms or kill them, over a 24-hour period of contact. The JIS Z 2801 procedure has been adopted as an International Organization for Standardization (ISO) procedure.

So, at this stage, it is a matter of watch this space. The antibacterial properties are likely to apply to a wider range of timbers than just spotted gum.

Use Standard Trade Names Only.

Care needs to be used when specifying a timber as it can be called by four possible names. These are:

- Botanical name
- Standard Trade Name
- Local name, and
- Marketing name

Botanical names. Few at the trade level and probably not too many at the supply level will be familiar working with botanical names. If these are being used, we recommend that they be used in conjunction with the Standard Trade Names. Remember also that some species are actually made up of a number of similar species. In the case of spotted gum, it is *Corymbia citriodora*, *Corymbia henryi* and *Corymbia maculata*. It is important to mention all three. They will be impossible to differentiate so there is no point introducing something that will be ignored, such as saying you will only accept *maculata*.

Standard trade names. These are the names that are used in conjunction with the botanical names in AS 5604, AS/NZS 1148 and CTIQ. These are the official names e.g., spotted gum.

Local names. The same trees can be called different things in different localities. E.g., forest red gum, and durability Class 1 in-ground timber is frequently called blue gum in Ted's home valley. One day a NSW logging contractor offered him a load of blue gum so he jumped at it. What turned up was Sydney blue gum, known in the locality it was drawn from as blue gum. The properties were vastly different. This has caused major problems on occasions and proves the merit of using both the botanical name in conjunction with the standard trade name.

Marketing names. A number of imported species are sold under names like "Pacific Tallowwood" "Pacific Spotted" and "Pacific Jarrah." Some of these timbers can be very good indeed (see the reference to cumaru/tonka in the species comparison in Table 7). Conversely, Ted has also seen two different species sold under one marketing name by two different suppliers. One was durable and the other was not. Designers should on no circumstance use this terminology unless combined with a botanical name. There may not be a standard trade name as the timber can have many different names depending on the country.

Why it is important to use the correct name.

It is vitally important to understand the potential consequence of not using Standard trade names in conjunction with a botanical name. Some time ago, Ted provided an expert witness report for a timber deck in Victoria that had gone badly wrong. The deck was specified to be supplied in F17 spotted gum or grey ironbark, both excellent and fit for purpose though the grade was too low (refer to the chapter *Timber Specification*). The contractor sought approval to use *grey gum*, another good and suitable species and when the Landscape Architect made independent enquiries, they were informed that, quite correctly, it was used by the Victorian government for jetty decking.

But "grey gum" as an Australian Standard trade name is *Eucalyptus propinqua var. propinqua* and *Eucalyptus punctata* but what was supplied was "mountain grey gum", with the botanical name *Eucalyptus cypellocarpa.* It was known locally to where it was milled as simply "grey gum." This timber is durability Class 3 and has 12% shrinkage. A high grade of this timber will still produce F17 which reinforced our position that specifying timber for exposed applications only by, or predominately by, F ratings is inadequate. Correspondence from the Landscape Architect included the following:

> At this present moment, the Client is ropeable due to the decking warping, cupping, and spaced between boards anywhere between 6 to 25 mm and screws being exposed by up to 8 mm. The specified maximum spacing was 6 mm at equilibrium moisture content and the screws countersunk 3 mm."

Our recommendation in the *Timber Specifications* is that you use both the standard trade name and the botanical names.

Imported Hardwood
As mentioned in the introduction to this guide, compliance to the playground standard is not likely to be a defence in the event of a claim due to poor timber performance or injury. Conversely, a timber may be fit for purpose even though it does not comply with the standard. This section looks at five imported species; kwila (merbau), larch, robinia, meranti, and rubberwood and discusses whether they should be

used in an Australian playground setting.

Kwila (Merbau)

One imported species has already been mentioned, kwila/merbau, a hardwood that has bushfire resistance and, being a durability Class 1 above-ground species in AS5604-2005 meets the requirements of AS4685.1-2021 for use in playgrounds. This timber has been used in Australia for decades and has proven successful in decking applications. Feedback and observations over many years has been that it is not as durable as the better Australian species, but it will perform well in a playground where the extreme longevity that is possible is not needed. Kwila should not be used for an in-ground application as then it is only durability Class 3.

Unfortunately, kwila/merbau has long been associated with illegal and unsustainable logging practices.

Figure 19.   Larch is used successfully in playgrounds in the UK

Larch

If you are a fan of the TV show Grand Designs, as Ted is, you would have heard the presenter wax lyrical about larch's durability. This conifer is sufficiently durable in the UK where a design life of 15 years can be achieved even with untreated sapwood.[34] There the climate and agents of attack are different from Australia but in our much harder conditions, larch would be very unsuitable.

Larch is not found in the species list in AS5604-2005 which the playground standard says to draw from, but it is found in an authoritative (and free) "go to" source for information, *Construction Timbers in Queensland*[35] and for anything in Queensland related to the Building Code, it is the Law, not a suggestion. This document draws on a wider range of reference material than is found in the Australian Standard and is adjusted for Australian conditions. This document classes larch as an in-ground and above-ground durability Class 4, i.e., the same as untreated radiata pine which even a novice would (hopefully) not use. To get some above-ground durability you need to treat it to Hazard 3, and if you have bolts close to the ground as in a stirrup, say 200 mm, in Ted's opinion that would be at least a Hazard 4 or even 5 which is, for all intents and purposes only available as CCA. This is not permitted in new playgrounds. The point is irrelevant as one importer is saying their material contains virtually no sapwood and you need at least a 12 mm envelope of sapwood to preserve the timber.

Note: A good source of information is the *Qtimber* website[36] which is an online searchable form of the CTIQ books. While this is a Queensland Government publication it is based on recognised Australian climatic zones (Figure 49) and so can be applied to any application that could be expected in the nation.

Robinia

Figure 20. Robinia, split and concreted in the ground.

Unlike kwila or larch, robinia is not mentioned in either AS5604-2005 or *Construction Timbers in Queensland* so there is no authoritative document that can be cited as to its Australian durability. Despite robinia's basic properties in our market being unknown, juvenile (early) growth[37] natural rounds have been gaining some popularity for use in playgrounds with one playground manufacturer describing them as "durable and [with] resistance to insects, fungus and inclement weather" and suitable for installation "in the ground

---

[34] Tom Hickman *Pers. Com.* 28 January 2021. Tom is Company Director with Playquip Leisure Ltd in the UK.
[35] Found at https://www.publications.qld.gov.au/dataset/construction-timbers-in-queensland.
[36] Queensland Government. *Qtimber*. URL: https://qtimber.daf.qld.gov.au/ Date Accessed: January 11, 2021.
[37] This represents the first 10 to 20 years of a robinia tree's growth. Dunisch, Oliver, Hans-Georg Richter, Gerald Koc. 2010. "Wood properties of juvenile and mature heartwood in Robinia pseudoacacia L.". *Wood Science and Technology Journal* 44:

without the need for chemical treatment."[38] This may well be the case in some countries but Ted has been contacted twice (at the time of writing) about Robinia splitting badly in playgrounds. Ted's opinion is that small diameter natural rounds are likely to be durability Class 3 at best for in-ground and above-ground rating. Sawn robinia from mature wood is likely to be higher. However, until someone puts the timber in the ground in different sites around Australia and makes L joints to gauge its above-ground durability it is all only opinion, however well informed. In an Australian setting, it is his belief there are better choices than robinia for playground equipment, and dare he say, far better choices. He bases this on its general durability, the use of juvenile wood in natural rounds,[39] potential for splintering and higher shrinkage than alternatives. The inability to apply an Australian durability class to robinia, in our opinion, makes it difficult, if not impossible to certify juvenile wood when used in playgrounds even when using the alternate methods provisions of the NCC.[40]

Consider the durability issue in more detail. Great claims are made about the durability of this species, but they are based on the European environment hence this should ring alarm bells for timber used in Australia. Under BS EN 350-2: 1994, the mature wood of robinia is classed as having class 1-2 resistance to fungi attack in Europe.[41] The four-tier durability scale used in Australia is different from that used in Europe and the UK. For instance, the UK uses a 5-tier system where it ranks Douglas fir (Oregon pine) as being a durability Class 3 species[42] meaning it is moderately durable with a life expectancy of 10 to 15 years. In Australia the same timber is durability Class 4 for in ground and above ground applications (the lowest rating) and in-ground it is only suitable for 0 to 5 years. Table 5 shows the different life expectancy of mature wood (not the juvenile wood which may be sold in natural rounds used in playgrounds) under different international ratings.

301.

[38] Proludic S.A,S. n.d. *Origin by proludic, Play value naturally*. (Vignon: Proludic. N.D.) 3.

[39] Dunisch. *Wood properties ...*, 301-313. The durability of juvenile wood in Europe can vary from a 2 to as low as a 4 on their 5-level scale depending on the decay mechanism i.e., from resistant to little resistant. Australian conditions are harsher.

[40] Refer NCC Volume 2, Section A2.2.

[41] British Standards Institution. *Durability of wood and wood-based products. Natural durability of solid wood. Guide to natural durability and treatability of selected wood species of importance in Europe*. (London: British Standards Institution. 1995) Reference 3.89. The standard was current till 2016.

[42] BS EN 350.2:1994, Table 4.

Class	1	2	3	4	5
	Probable life in years[43]				
Aust above-ground[44]	> 40	15 to 40	7 to 15	0 to 7	
Aust in-ground[45]	> 25	15 to 25	5 to 15	0 to 5	
UK[46]	>25	15-25	10-15	5-10	<5
EU[47]	?	?	?	?	?
China[48]	> 9	6 to 8	2 to 5	< 2	
Japan[49]	> 9	7 to 8.5	5 to 6.5	3 to 4.5	< 2.5
Malaysia[50]	> 10	5 to 10	2 to 5	< 2	
Bangladesh[51]	> 3	2 to 3	1 to 2	< 1	
Tanzania[52]	> 10	5 to 10	2 to 5	1 to 2	< 1
Brazil[53]	> 8	5 to 8	2 to 5	< 2	
USA[54]	?	?	?	?	
Canada	?	?	?	?	

Table 6. . Different international durability scales.

Meranti

We are aware that "meranti of the Shorea species"[55] is used by at least one manufacturer for use in playgrounds. It was described as a light hardwood that is "Durable and resistant to insect attack." By defining it as meranti of the *Shorea* group it is differentiated from light and dark red meranti which can

---

[43] A considerable degree of caution should be exercised with these expected life expectancies, particularly for unpainted horizontal surfaces.
[44] Standards. AS 5604-2005 …, Table 1.
[45] Standards. AS 5604-2005 …, Table 1.
[46] The durability classes in BS EN 350-1 are now termed DC1 to DC5. The service lives are from the Building Research Establishment's *A Handbook of Softwoods* last edition published in 1977, now out of print. Sycamore, Janet. Pers Com. 25 April 2018. There aren't separate classifications for in and above ground applications
[47] Despite the same standard being used in Europe as in the UK, the same expectancy does not apply. At the time of writing there is no uniform "European approach to link durability classes to service lives or service life categories" nor is there agreement on these categories. Brischke, Christian. *Pers. Com.* 12 June 2021. Contact the writer for further information.
[48] Stirling, Rod. *Natural Durability Classification Systems Used Around the World*. Paper presented at The International Research Group on Wood Protection conference, Beijing, China May 2009. Reference: IRG/WP 09-10694, 5.
[49] Stirling. *Natural* …, 6.
[50] Stirling. *Natural* …, 6.
[51] Stirling. *Natural* …, 6.
[52] Stirling. *Natural* …, 6.
[53] Stirling. *Natural* …, 6.
[54] Timber durability standards in the USA and Canada are less evolved than in Australia and Europe and there no standards for natural durability similar to AS 5604. Stirling. Natural …, 4-5.
[55] Forpark. n.d. *Essentials*. Accessed March 6, 2021. https://www.forparkaust.com.au/wp-content/uploads/2019/09/Essentials-Material-Specifications-2019.pdf.

be from the *Copaifera* spp., *Larix* spp, and *Sindora* spp groups.[56] Timbers from all of these can also be termed "meranti".

Construction Timbers in Queensland lists only four "merantis" drawn from the *Shorea* spp group, light red, dark red, yellow and white. They are all classed as durability Class 4 in- above-ground situations and the best in-ground is Class 3 making them all unfit for playground use. Preservation is unlikely to be successful in gaining the necessary penetration. Only yellow meranti has termite resistance. They also have very low strength.

Rubberwood

Very similar things apply to rubberwood (*Hevea brasiliensis*as) has been said about Meranti. It is not mentioned in AS 5604 but is found in CTIQ where it is listed as an inground durability Class 4 and, above-ground, is provisionally a Class 4. It is not termite resistant. It also has the lowest strength group, when unseasoned, a 7, and almost the lowest, 7 on a scale of 1 to 8 for dry. Rubberwood is not termite resistant either. It is not suitable for playgrounds though we have seen it used in this application.

---

[56] CTIQ: Book 2. Meranti is dealt with more comprehensively in CTIQ than in AS 5604.

This page is intentionally blank

Species	Percentage of harvest from Qld State forests[57]	Percentage of harvest from NSW State forests[58]	Fire resistance AS 3959-2009	Termite resistant AS5604-2005	Lyctus susceptible AS5604-2005	In-ground Durability AS5604-2005 or CTIQ	Above-ground Durability AS5604-2005 or CTIQ
Ash silvertop *E. sieberi*	NSW/Vic/Tas	0.12	Y	N	N	3	2
Ash Victorian *E. delegatensis E. regnans*	Vic		N	N	Y[59]	4	3
Blackbutt *E. pilularis*	4.58	15.84	Y	Y	N	2	1
Box Grey *E moluccana*	1.57	0.08	N	Y	Y	1	1
Brigalow *Acacia harpophylla*			N	Y	Y	1	1
Cumaru/Tonka *Dipteryx odorata*	Imported		N	N	Y	(1)	(1)
Cypress white *Callitris glauca*			N	Y	N	2	1
Ironbark broadleaved red *E. fibrosa*	7.02	2.01[60]	N	Y	N	1	1

---

[57] Based on figures 2003 to 2013 from state forests and grazing leases and not expected to change in the short term. Seibuhr, Jane. *Pers. Com.* 12 February 2015.
[58] Based on 2013-4 financial year and expected to be constant for 10 years. Grealy, Martin. *Pers. Com.* 13 July 2015.
[59] AS5604-2005 A3.2 notes that Victorian origin Victorian Ash is not susceptible but this requires absolute certainty in purchasing.
[60] Includes grey, mugga and broadleaf ironbark which are not lyctus resistant.

Species	Playground use in-ground AS4685 or CTIQ	Playground use above-ground AS4685 or CTIQ	Interlocked grain[61]	Dry weight kg/m3	Shrinks tangential to 12% MC	Greasy to touch	Royal species
Ash silvertop *E. sieberi*	N	Y	O	820	10.6	N	N
Ash Victorian *E. delegatensis E. regnans*	N	N	N	680	8-13	N	N
Blackbutt *E. pilularis*	Y	Y	N	930	7.3	N	N
Box Grey *E moluccana*	Y	Y	N	1105	7.5	N	N
Brigalow *Acacia harpophylla*	Y	Y	N	1025	3	N	N
Cumaru/Tonka *Dipteryx odorata*	Y	Y	?	900-1300	7.7	N	
Cypress white *Callitris glauca*	Y	Y	N	675	3	N	N
Ironbark broadleaved red *E. fibrosa*	Y	Y	O	1120	6.5	N	Y

---

[61] Information not drawn from the listed Australian Standards, other than royal species is drawn from Keith Bootle's *Wood in Australia* and Department of Primary Industries *Timber Species Notes*. Royal species list is drawn from industry knowledge.

Species	Percentage of harvest from Qld State forests[62]	Percentage of harvest from NSW State forests[63]	Fire resistance AS 3959-2009	Termite resistant AS5604-2005	Lyctus susceptible AS5604-2005	In-ground Durability AS5604-2005 or CTIQ	Above-ground Durability AS5604-2005 or CTIQ
Ironbark narrowleaved red *E. crebra*	4.60		N	Y	N	1	1
Ironbark red *E. sideroxylon*	Not listed		Y	Y	Y	1	1
Ironbark Grey *E. paniculata*	4.45		N	Y	N	1	1
Gum river red *E, camaldulensis*	Not common in Qld	5.41	Y	Y	Y	2	1
Gum spotted *C. maculata & C. citrodora* *E. henryi*	68.81	5.9	Y	Y	Y	2	1
Kwila (merbau) *Intsia bijuga*	Imported		Y	Y	Y	3	1
Mahogany White *E acmenoides*	1.42	0.047	N	N	N	1	1
Messmate Gympie *E. cloeziana*	1.23		N	N	N	1	1
Tallowwood *E. microcorys*	0.92	1.27	N	Y	N	1	1

---

[62] Based on figures 2003 to 2013 from state forests and grazing leases and not expected to change in the short term. Seibuhr, Jane. Pers. Com. 12 February 2015.

[63] Based on 2013-4 financial year and expected to be constant for 10 years. Grealy, Martin. *Pers. Com.* 13 July 2015.

Species	Playground use in-ground AS4685 or CTIQ	Playground use above-ground AS4685 or CTIQ	Interlocked grain[64]	Dry weight kg/m3	Shrinks tangential to 12% MC	Greasy to touch	Royal species
Ironbark narrowleaved red *E. crebra*	Y	Y	Y	1090	5	N	Y
Ironbark red *E. sideroxylon*	Y	Y	Y	1190	7	N	Y
Ironbark Grey *E. paniculata*	Y	Y	O	1105	7.5	N	Y
Gum river red *E, camaldulensis*	Y	Y	Y	895	8	N	N
Gum spotted *C. maculata & C. citrodora E. henryi*	Y	Y	O	1010	6.1	Y	Y[65]
Kwila (merbau) *Intsia bijuga*	N	Y	N	865	2.6	O	N
Mahogany White *E acmenoides*	Y	Y	O	1010	6	N	N
Messmate Gympie *E. cloeziana*	Y	Y	N	1010	6	N	Y
Tallowwood *E. microcorys*	Y	Y	O	1010	6.1	Y	Y

---

[64] Information not drawn from the listed Australian Standards, other than royal species is drawn from Keith Bootle's *Wood in Australia* and Department of Primary Industries *Timber Species Notes*. Royal species list is drawn from industry knowledge.

[65] Above ground applications only

Species	Percentage of harvest from Qld State forests[66]	Percentage of harvest from NSW State forests[67]	Fire resistance AS 3959-2009	Termite resistant AS5604-2005	Lyctus susceptible AS5604-2005	In-ground Durability AS5604-2005 or CTIQ	Above-ground Durability AS5604-2005 or CTIQ
Robinia[68] *Robinia pseudoacacia*	imported		N	N?	?[69]	(3)[70]	(3)
Turpentine *Syncarpia glomulifera*	0.11	0.25	Y	Y	N	2	1

---

[66] Based on figures 2003 to 2013 from state forests and grazing leases and not expected to change in the short term. Seibuhr, Jane. Pers. Com. 12 February 2015.
[67] Based on 2013-4 financial year and expected to be constant for 10 years. Grealy, Martin. *Pers. Com.* 13 July 2015.
[68] The Wood Database. *Black Locust*. URL: http://www.wood-database.com/black-locust/ Date accessed: 26 January 2018
[69] Normally sold with sapwood removed so lyctus is not going to be an issue
[70] Not listed in AS 4685 or CTIQ and has never been tested in Australia. This is Ted's informed opinion of the mature wood.

Species	Playground use in-ground AS4685 or CTIQ	Playground use above-ground AS4685 or CTIQ	Interlocked grain[71]	Dry weight kg/m3	Shrinks tangential to 12% MC	Greasy to touch	Royal species
Robinia[72] *Robinia pseudoacacia*	N	N	N	660-790	7.2	N	N
Turpentine *Syncarpia glomulifera*	Y	Y	O	945	13	N	N

Table 7. Properties of some Australian and imported timbers.

Legend

Ted prefers these species for above-ground **sawn** use

Ted prefers these species for both inground and above **sawn** ground use

Ted prefers these species for **natural round** use

G = Generally, N = No, O = Often, S = Sometimes, Y = Yes,

---

[71] Information not drawn from the listed Australian Standards, other than royal species is drawn from Keith Bootle's *Wood in Australia* and Department of Primary Industries *Timber Species Notes*. Royal species list is drawn from industry knowledge.

[72] The Wood Database. *Black Locust*. URL: http://www.wood-database.com/black-locust/ Date accessed: 26 January 2018

Figure 21.   Large, high shelters are needed for playgrounds[73]

The guidance that follows in this book assumes that the playground is in the full Australian sun. When timber is not exposed to the weather, say under a roof or even heavily shaded by trees the stresses on the timber are far less. Notwithstanding, we would not adjust the design practices.

Conclusion

There are many complex considerations when choosing a suitable timber species for playground applications. There is no perfect species, just as there is no perfect material for building playgrounds as alternatives to timber come with their own problems e.g., steel rusts and plastic degrades etc. But despite that, incredibly good timber options are available. If you start with an understanding that our Australian climate is very harsh and will not forgive any oversights in design and add to that an appreciation that playground timbers require properties far exceeding those of framing timbers, you are well along the path to specifying timber well. Certain (royal) species have a long track record of use in weather exposed applications such as bridge construction and can be relied on to perform very well if the grade is correct and the detailing is correct.

---

[73] This shelter marketed by Ted and developed in conjunction with Timber Restoration Services had a 4 metre clearance at the posts and 6 metre at the apex and covered 14 metre. Normal park shelters are far too small.

2 SAWN TIMBER IN PLAYGROUNDS

Introduction
The timber market is geared around the mass supply of domestic framing such as stud frame walls, roof framing and trusses, floor framing, verandah framing and joists. There bulk quantities are sold, and the only matter of consideration are the structural properties at the time of processing and treatment for very low risk (H1 and H2) situations. This timber is likely to be used with little thought to placement and as quickly as possible in a truss and frame operation as it has already been through a grading process, either visual or mechanical. Once erected, the walls and ceilings are covered with sheeting and topped off, most likely, with a metal roof. A critical eye will never see what the timber looks like and so pass comment on the aesthetics. Further, apart from decks and verandah floors, with no wetting and drying there is no impact on the fasteners and nailplates and there is no corrosion. With adequate termite protection, and providing there are no leaks, even the lowest durability timber can perform as intended for hundreds of years regardless of the type and extent of the natural characteristics present.

The needs of playground timber cannot be further removed from that of housing. It is Ted's opinion that the main reason for the loss of confidence in timber for use in playgrounds has been caused by the use of general framing timbers in this application. There can be a conflict when the engineers primary concern is strength at the time of construction when the critical consideration is ongoing durability.[75] Timber of high durability, either by natural or chemical means, and of

Species	% strength remaining
Jarrah	75
Sydney blue gum	60
Spotted gum	48
Grey ironbark	38

Table 8.   F14 as a percentage of the green off saw strength of solid timber of that same species.[74]

the best quality is required to build a successful playground. Whereas timber for framing is specified by strength, playground timber must be specified by careful attention to the species and by a description of what the timber actually looks like.

How should we understand a specification that simply says "F14 hardwood"? *AS2082-2007 Timber - Hardwood - Visually stress-graded for structural purposes* describes four qualities of timber called "Structural Grades". This can be confused with the term "Proof Grade", but they are not the same thing. These four structural grades describe what the timber looks like and represent a percentage of the strength of that species when it is free of defects. These rules enable the timber grader, with no more than a tape measure, to classify a piece of timber into one of the four grades or to reject it altogether as not being suitable for a structural application. These are not subjective but pass/fail assessments without any grey areas. The F rating or the "proof grade" is then assessed by comparing the percentage of strength remaining (Structural Grade) to the properties of an individual species and this varies considerably. Table 8 shows that F14 hardwood could be supplied in a high-quality piece of jarrah but this is an above-ground two species and Ted questions the suitability of this, or a very low-quality piece of grey ironbark, equally unsuitable. Should the specification be for kiln dried timber then generally it would be that that same piece

---

[74] AS 2082-2008. Table A2.
[75] Guidance is given in the chapter on specifications on how to harmonise these two viewpoints.

jumps two grades and that low-quality grey ironbark then becomes a piece of F22, and the jarrah is also F22.[76] F14 kiln dried timber would be of such poor quality it would generally be off the scale (in the wrong way) for any hardwood that was considered usable in a protected house frame. The process Ted has described with hardwood is similar to that of visually graded pine and cypress and the same difficulties arise when specifying those timbers only by F grades for playgrounds.

The chapter *Timber Specification* outlies what we believed is necessary to be supplied to provide a successful structure in sawn and round timber and is a summary of this and the following chapter. What follows in this Chapter is intended to allow the designer to understand the considerations that apply when using sawn timber in playgrounds and provide the basis for the specification. These tighter specifications above simple structural issues are necessary. A designer cannot expect to receive timber on site than is any better than what he/she has specified, especially when it is being supplied by the lowest tenderer.

What About Kiln Dried Timber?
As mentioned in the Chapter *Standards and Fitness for Purpose*, solid pine is generally only available in kiln dried but then only in limited widths, i.e., 35 and 45 mm. Cypress, which is available in a bigger range of sizes is low shrinkage (3%) and it would make little sense to kiln dry it and is probably not available dry anyway. The complication is only with hardwood. Over the years Ted has seen playground designs with 150x150 mm and 200x200 mm kiln dried specified. The expression is used as a throwaway line without any understanding that it is simply not available. When designing with hardwood you cannot avoid the necessity of learning how to accommodate shrinkage. These sizes generally cannot be supplied dry from recycled timber. When cut from larger sizes such as girders and powerpoles they behave just like green off saw (GOS) timber. The original piece was simply too large to dry. These large sizes in hardwood dry (perhaps stabilise is a better word) at about 25 mm per year so the only sure way of obtaining a 150x150 hardwood seasoned is to put it in the weather for six years!!!

What About Recycled Timber?

Specifying recycled hardwood may give the designer and the customer "warm and fuzzy feelings" about saving the planet but the complications it introduces may not be worth it. As mentioned, recycled timber is no guarantee that the timber will be dry but there are further and more serious implications.

---

[76] AS 2082-2008, Table A1.

Recycled timber of an appropriate species in basically their original sawn sizes and taken from a demolished house or warehouse etc., e/g. joists and bearers, or recycled hardwood decking, properly de-nailed should generally be suitable for playgrounds. The only limitation is that non lyctus susceptible timber is likely not to have the sapwood treated, and treating old timber is unsuccessful.

Increasingly however, larger sections are being cut from powerpoles that have been withdrawn from service. They are CCA treated and of small dimension. Accepting a 200x200 mm post from such timber would be very unwise due to its propensity to split as can be seen in Figure 22. Splitting in a smaller size such as a 150x150 mm would be even more severe. But critically, the image shows CCA treatment on the outside making such timber totally unsuitable for playgrounds. It could (and indeed, should) result in very expensive rectification expenses.

Figure 22.   200x200 mm recycled timber containing CCA treatment.

It is Ted's opinion that designers are safer ignoring larger section recycled timber altogether unless there is a system of independent inspection that there is no CCA.

Considerations When Specifying Sawn Timber
The next chapter discusses round timber which is an entirely different material to sawn and can look and behave very differently. Generally speaking, when a tree has an injury it protects itself by growing over that injury and you then can't see what is inside. But when it is sawn you are dealing with timber, warts and all, with all the hidden natural features visible and exposed to the weather. It is possible that without correct specification and supply that you may be presented with a piece of timber that has heart in the centre, sapwood on the outside and heartwood in-between (Figure 23) and an excessive amount of natural feature. The previous chapter which deals with standards and fitness for purpose has explained and illustrated these terms.

Larger sizes, for all intents and purposes are the preserve of hardwood as the log size is generally larger than that of cypress and pine. Sizes as large as 200x200 are readily available. The maximum size recommended for cypress is in the range of 125x125 mm to 175x175mm with 125x125 mm being the most readily available. Larger sections (200x200 mm to 300x300) have very limited availability and a much more limited length range.[77] Untreated sapwood is going to be an issue with these sizes too. Pine mills are generally not geared up to produce large section sizes and most production, other than landscaping grades, which are unsuitable for playgrounds is turned into 35 and 45 mm framing.

---

[77] Wildman, Errol. *Pers. Com.* 2 January 2021.

Heart

Heart in hardwood in sizes up to 150x150 mm

Figure 23. 150x150 hardwood post with untreated sapwood on edges and heart in the centre.

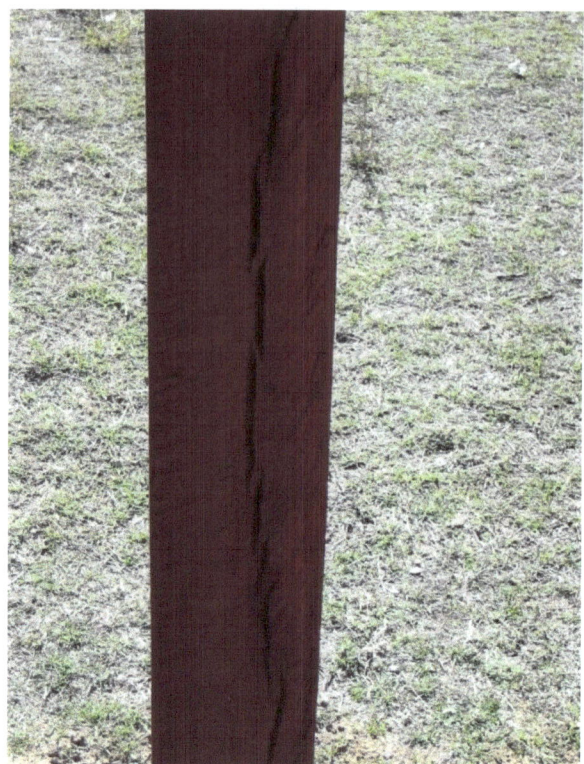

Figure 24. Checking in the heartwood caused by included heart are large enough to be finger entrapments

Sizes up to 150x150 mm **must** be supplied free of heart and this can be difficult given the diminishing log size over recent years. This recommendation follows the requirements of AS2082-2000[78] and the current guidelines of *AS3818,7-2010 Timber - Heavy structural products - Visually graded, Part 7: Large cross-section sawn hardwood engineering timbers* for select grade timber.[79] This recommendation is discussed in detail as Sin Number 3 in Ted's book, *The Seven Deadly Sins of External Timber Design*. The difficulties in supplying this timber free of heart should cause designers to avoid this size and limit it to 125x125 mm and even then, it should be specified free of heart. If heart is included, the piece should be at least 200x200 mm to reduce the possibility of splitting.

From Figure 23 and Figure 24 a designer can understand the type of material that is on the market and the need for careful specification and, along with that, independent confirmation grading. The post in Figure 23, sawn from one of the ironbarks, is from a stem that is so small that the wane of the log is seen on two edges and the heart is boxed in the centre. The other image, taken only a month after sawing shows that

---

[78] AS 2802-2000, 2.1.2 (e). This was changed in the later standard but came with a warning.
[79] AS 3818,7-2010 *Timber - Heavy structural products - Visually graded, Part 7: Large cross-section sawn hardwood engineering timbers*, 3.2 (f) (i) (A).

timber containing heart can split so badly that finger entrapments are possible.[80] Splits allow weather into the timber and reduce life so it is important for finger entrapment issues.

Heart in hardwood for sizes over 150x150 mm

It is simply impossible to produce sawn timber free of heart in sizes over 150x150 mm. Ted's experience is that 175x175 mm should be avoided as it is still prone to split and, as mentioned, he advised going to timber with a minimum size of 200x200 mm. This means that 200x150 mm is unsuitable as splitting is almost certain to occur, as shown in Figure 25.

Figure 25.   200x150 recycled   Figure 26.   192x192 Pioneer post

Cracking associated with the heart can be controlled simply with the use of expansion joints but there must be more than one. Shown in Figure 26 is a product developed by Ted called the "Pioneer post" which features three expansion joints, a pencil round into the joint and pencil rounded corners.[81] It is finished a uniform size at 192x192. Unless the post is situated under a roof, capping is essential

---

[80] Ted and Ralph use the term "finger entrapment" in the sense of fitness for purpose rather than strictly according to the wording of the standard. The difference is discussed in the chapter, *Inspection and Maintenance*, under *Finger entrapment associated with splits*

[81] While the design is not protected, tooling costs and the availability of planers that will process 200x200 mm means it will have limited availability. It is available as a standard product through Wilson Timbers/Outdoor Structures Australia and now has four grooves.

Heart in cypress, all sizes.

Figure 27. The heart of cypress (and pine) must be protected

Figure 28. Metal cap used to protect the heart of cypress.

Both the heartwood and heart of cypress are durability Class 2 in-ground, though it was formerly classified as durability Class 1, meaning it is borderline between the two. Cypress also has lower shrinkage (3%) than most hardwoods, and certainly when compared to the species that are more readily available in larger sizes such as spotted gum (6.1%) and narrow leafed red ironbark (5%). Unlike the heart of hardwood, that of cypress is stable and does not produce the checking shown in Figure 24 through to Figure 25 meaning there is no limitation to the sizes that can include it. As the log size is generally smaller than hardwood it is unrealistic to specify larger sizes without heart as discussed under *Considerations with sawn timber* above. The heart will deteriorate when used as posts (Figure 27) and must be capped to give a long-term maintenance free life (Figure 28).

Heart in pine, all sizes.

Like cypress, the heart of pine is stable and can be included in house framing without any limitation when structural issues are the only consideration. Unlike cypress, the heart is not durable, and it cannot be made durable by chemical means (Figure 7) without the timber being incised (Figure 8). The extent of heart in any given piece is very small and will normally be combined with timber that is predominantly heartwood. If sawn pine with more than 10% heart and heartwood and not available incised to the correct depth, and it is highly unlikely it will be, a case cannot be made for the use of this timber in playgrounds. If a suitable product can be found, the ends of posts must be capped, as with cypress.

Heartwood

Hardwood, all sizes

As discussed in the chapter on *Standards and Fitness for Purpose*, the heartwood of some species is extremely durable in-ground while others have similar durability above-ground. The species that Ted considers more appropriate are highlighted in Table 5. Providing a suitable species is selected for the application, there are no restrictions in using the heartwood of hardwood. Posts that do not include heart do not need to be capped but must be detailed to shed moisture.

Cypress, all sizes

Like the heart, the heartwood of cypress is extremely durable and can be used without any restrictions. Care needs to be taken with inground applications as outlined in the chapter *Engaging with the Ground*. It is unlikely that it will be possible to purchase a piece large enough to meet the requirement for given service life for embedded timber outlined in *Construction Timbers in Queensland*.

Pine, all sizes

The same restrictions apply to the heartwood of pine as with the heart. Unless it is incised to the required depth, or the heartwood/heart content does not exceed 10% this product is not suitable for use in playgrounds.

Sapwood

Sapwood in hardwood, all sizes

Providing the preservatives prohibited in *AS4685.1* are not used, there is no limit to the amount of hardwood sapwood permitted. The sapwood of hardwood is easy to treat to H3 for above-ground applications but not so for H4 and H5 applications which require pre-drying. Untreated sapwood should not be used under any circumstance.

Sapwood in cypress, all sizes

The sapwood of cypress cannot be treated so its inclusion needs to be limited to a maximum of 10% (20% if painted in southern states) to minimise the likelihood of finger entrapment. All sapwood, whether hardwood, Cypress or pine is classed as durability Class 4, whether in-ground or above-ground but has a long history of use outside of the tropics as painted chamfer board house cladding but when used without a paint coating it will decay. Generally, playgrounds do not have a paint coating which is known to protect the sapwood, especially in southern markets but will not be successful in North Queensland. It is better to limit the amount of sapwood as when it decays it will not look attractive and can produce finger entrapments but be prepared to pay extra for the timber.

Sapwood in pine, all sizes

The sapwood of pine is readily treatable and there is no restriction on the amount permitted. In larger sizes however it is unlikely that it will be free of heartwood and unless incised, it is necessary that the piece be at least 90% sapwood.

Natural feature

General

It is impossible to purchase timber, whether hardwood, cypress, or pine, free of natural feature but it is possible to specify it so that only a small amount is intended to be supplied. Limiting the amount of natural feature is important as, generally, when they are exposed to the weather they deteriorate further. Australian Standards have limited suitability for playground timber, and they require some modification. The guidance below is intended to describe what a piece of timber looks like not how strong it is.

Hardwood other than decking

Irrespective of the species, any timber intended for use in the framing, but not decking, should be supplied to Structural Grade 1 to AS2082. In addition, there should be minimal tight gum vein and tight gum veins on two face intersecting an edge (Figure 29) should be excluded. Table 9 shows the different F grades that can be achieved in different species from Structural Grade 1. To understand what this timber looks like, a simplified version of the grade limits is given in Table 10.

Figure 29.   Gum vein on two faces intersecting an edge must not be used

Producing from the following species		
	Unseasoned	Seasoned
Tallowwood	F27	F34
Spotted gum	F22	F34
Sydney blue gum	F17	F27
Jarrah	F14	F22

Table 9.   F grades that can be produced from Structural Garde 1 hardwood

Fault	Permitted extent
Fractures and splits	Only end splits are allowed
Sawing Tolerance	+ or – 3 mm
Knots	One seventh of face
Borer holes	12 per 100x100 mm (up to 3 mm)
Termite galleries	Enclosed - not permitted, open - as for want and wane
Slope of grain	1 in 15 (jarrah 1 in 12)
Heart[82]	Not permitted where smaller dimension under 175 mm. Limited to inner one third for other sizes. Permitted in limited species[83] to be one twentieth of cross section.
Tight gum veins	Max one and a half times the length in aggregate. One quarter the length if extending face to face. Ted's additional requirement – not intersecting an edge
Loose gum veins and included bark	One tenth the length and 3 mm max measured radially. Not extending from face to face
Gum pockets	Up to three times the width to a max. 300 mm. On one face, a quarter of the width up to 12 mm
End splits	The width but exceeding 100 mm in aggregate (per end)
Checks	Up to 3 mm wide and one quarter the length
Rot	3 mm deep and 150x100 mm per 2.0m length
Want and wane, Lyctus susceptible sapwood	One tenth of the cross section

Table 10.   Structural Grade 1 hardwood (simplified rules)[84]

An engineer will want to do calculations based on an F grade, so Ted recommend that he/she looks at the list of species the designer has allowed and takes the one with the lowest strength group for either green or dry whichever is the application. If the specification does not have independent verification of grade,

---

[82] Refer to notes Included Heart where the implications of the change of definition of heart in AS 2082 are discussed in detail.
[83] These are blackbutt, grey box, forest red gum, spotted gum, grey ironbark, broad and narrow leaved red ironbark.
[84] From AS 2082 -2007 2.1

then assume the timber will be supplied to one grade lower than is specified.[85] That will give a minimum F grade that will be received. It is then important that you do not have contradictory specifications of an F rating that has come from the engineer and a physical description from the architect. The plans should include wording something like, "The calculations for this playground are based on F17 hardwood. The physical descriptions of the timber will meet and most likely exceed F17. Timber is to be supplied to the physical descriptions, not to the F ratings."

Hardwood, decking kiln dried

All 19 mm hardwood decking must be kiln dried. The requirements for Select grade[86] light decking to *AS2796.2 Timber—Hardwood—Sawn and milled products Part 2: Grade description* can be used with little modification when combined with an appropriate species. This standard describes decking with almost a clear face and with a maximum knot of 15mm and that must be tight. The only modification would be that the timber should be free of tight gum vein intersecting an edge and face.

Thicker decking, with a nominal dimension of 35 or 45 mm can be supplied but there could be a 3-month delay (at least) in the supply. The same standard applies. This material should not be confused with the more readily available F22 kiln dried Australian hardwood which has a very generous allowance for natural feature. To upgrade from framing to decking will probably require the contractor to order 30% extra material – refer to the case history on the Arab dhow.

Hardwood, decking green off saw.

Hardwood decking that is a nominal 35 or 45 mm can be supplied unseasoned but, as with kiln dried framing, the allowance for timber framing is too generous to be used as decking, especially in playgrounds. Ted developed a commercial decking called Deckwood which has its own specification but briefly it was intended to have an almost clear face. While there are restrictions on the shape of Deckwood there is no such issues with the timber specification. It is reproduced in the timber specification.

When using unseasoned hardwood of suitable species, the timber is laid without a gap and it develops as the sun dries the timber. The very widest that should be used is 120 mm which in spotted gum will shrink 6% or 7.2 mm. Ted's preference for playgrounds would be 90-95mm.

Cypress

General

Cypress is visually graded to *AS2858 - Timber - Softwood - Visually stress-graded for structural purposes.* An appropriate grade would be F7, the highest of the three grades given in the standard, and there is merit in adding Structural Appearance Grade though this may make supply too difficult. To understand what cypress graded to F7 looks like, We have summarised the grading rules in Table 11

---

[85] AS 2082-2007 1.10.3 allows that 5% of a parcel can be one grade lower than specified.
[86] AS 2796.2-1999, A2.

Fault	Permitted extent
Fractures and splits	Only end splits are allowed
Sawing Tolerance	+2 or -4mm
Knots	Face - average of two faces – 30%
	Edge – average of two edges – 50%
	Arris – average of the two faces, 20%
Borer holes	20 per 100x100 mm (up to 3 mm)
Termite galleries	Enclosed - not permitted, open - as for want and wane
Slope of grain	1 in 8
Heart	No limit
Tight and loose gum veins	Not a characteristic of cypress
Resin and bark pockets	150 mm long, 10mm width (measured radially)
End splits	The lesser of the face width or 100 mm
Checks	Unlimited
Rot	Not permitted
Want and wane,	20% of cross section and maximum 50% of the edge if 50mm thick

Table 11. F7 cypress (simplified rules)[87]

To achieve F7 in 38 mm cypress is more difficult than with 50 mm as the amount of sapwood on the edge is limited to 33%. It is Ted's opinion that sizes under 50 mm should be avoided.

Pine

General

Plantation pine is available, at least theoretically, both visually graded and machine proof graded (MPG). For sizes up to 45 mm all that may be available is MPG timber. Larger sizes are only supplied visually graded. Like hardwood, there are Structural Grades which describe what the timber looks like, except that there are five grades, not four. Ideally, the timber should be specified as visually graded to Structural Grade 1 to *AS2858 Timber—Softwood—Visually stressgraded for structural purposes*. If visual grading is not available then use MGP15, the highest machine proof grade available. The relationship between F and MGP grades is given in Table 12.

F Grade	MGP Substitute
F5	MGP10
F8	MGP12
F11	MGP15

Table 12. Relation of F to MGP grades[88]

---

[87] From AS 2858-1999, 1.7.1, Section 3.
[88] Queensland Government. *Qtimber, Strength groups and stress grades*. URL: https://qtimber.daf.qld.gov.au/guides/strength-groups-and-stress-grades Date Accessed: January 11, 2021.

Species	F grade
Radiata	F8
Slash	F14
Hoop	F8
Douglas Fir	F11

Table 13. F grades produced from the highest visual grade[89]

Like hardwood the highest visual grades will produce different F grades depending on the species (Table 13). And likewise, it is necessary that the designer ensure that there is not a contradiction between their physical description and the engineer's specification e.g., the designer may be expecting a high-quality piece of radiata pine (Structural Grade 1) but may receive a low-quality piece of slash pine (Structural Grade 4). The plans should include wording something like, "The calculations for this playground are based on F8 pine. The physical descriptions of the timber will meet and most likely exceed F8. Timber is to be supplied to the physical descriptions, not to the F ratings. To understand what pine to this grade looks like, we have summarised the grading rules in Table 11

Fault	Permitted extent
Fractures and splits	Only end splits are allowed
Sawing Tolerance	+-3 mm
Knots	In central half of face or edge – average of both sides,25%
	Other – average of the two faces, 15%
Borer holes	10 per 100x100 mm (up to 3 mm)
Termite galleries	Not permitted
Slope of grain	1 in 15
Heart	No limit
Tight and loose gum veins	Not a characteristic of plantation pine
Resin and bark pockets	Not permitted
End splits	Not permitted
Checks	Up to 2 mm wide, 450 mm long.
Rot	Not permitted
Want and wane,	10% of cross section and maximum 33% of the edge if 50mm thick

Table 14. Structural Grade 1 pine (simplified rules)[90]

Pine decking

Due to its propensity to splinter, we would not recommend pine for decking or any other horizontal application, e.g., handrail.

Surface Finish

Timber is generally available as rough sawn or dressed. Availability will be limited in plantation pine to dressed or rougher headed[91] but the designer will have a choice in hardwood and cypress. Rough sawn will weather better than dressed and absorb oil (such as Tanacoat) better than dressed timber. An additional

---

[89] AS 2858-1999 Table A1 and Section 4. Hoop is graded to different rules to plantation pine.
[90] From AS 2858-1999, Section 2 and 1.7.1.
[91] Rougher headed is when the timber has fine micro- reeds which assist with the adhesion of the plasterboard glue.

buff with a wire brush on an angle grinder to a rough sawn finish also assists if there is any question. Splinters are seldom an issue if the edges are pencil rounded.

Independent Verification of Grade

There is considerable variability among suppliers and if the purchasing process involves getting a price from three suppliers, too often the contract is awarded to the supplier with the highest non-conformance. The designer should be aware that there is no timber industry wide system of verification that visually graded timber has actually been supplied to grade. Ted's experience is that when the timber is purchased on price rather than from a trusted supplier, there is a real chance (if not inevitability) of timber not being supplied to grade. If non-conforming timber arrives on site, you can be assured it will be used! It would be rare for the builder to understand what he/she is looking[92] or have done a grading course or delay the build while replacement timber is delivered.

Figure 30. Ted grading timber intended for seats

We would urge the designer to have part of his specification independent verification of grade. This involves an outside person looking at all four sides of each piece of timber and accepting or rejecting it.

---

[92] Ted has written a useful guide *Grading Hardwood – Understanding AS 2082*. It illustrates the natural feature that will be encountered and explains how that can impact timber performance when exposed to the weather.

3 ROUND TIMBER IN PLAYGROUNDS

Introduction
There are very good reasons for using round timber, and particularly natural rounds instead of sawn as the main elements of a playground. Instead of "cooky cutter" playground items each piece is handmade and individual. This combined with the bumps and bends provide a rustic look which add to the nature play experience. If supplied with appropriate timber and well built, such a playground can have improved longevity, simply because the timber sizes are larger. But also, there are very good reasons why not to use such material. Poor species choice and detailing can see increased splitting and splintering. As well, if the sapwood is not removed or treated, the timber can quickly deteriorate, and the items need replacing far earlier that would be hoped. The down sides of round timber can be avoided if care is taken in the design, specification and supply and construction of playgrounds using round timber.

When Ted first started treating pine rounds, the product was very basic. The small diameter pine plantation thinnings were run through a debarking machine leaving, at least theoretically, the natural surface of the pine. In reality, the process was brutal and damage from the de-barker could be severe with considerable burring and potential for splinters. For these to be made suitable for playground use it would have required considerable work. How often this work was done is debatable, but the timber was certainly used in playgrounds. Fortunately, we have moved on from that with any modern pine playgrounds generally utilising parallel sided round timber though it should be noted that some of this old material may well be in service and should be considered during inspections.

Round timber can bring with it its own problems simply because they are not round. At best they are "roundish" but in truth they are irregularly shaped. In addition, they taper along the length and are not straight. This was dealt with in pine by passing the raw post through a rounding machine which produces dead straight, parallel sided posts which could be treated and they had a very long life indeed.[93] While the debarked rounds may have had, at times, too much character the parallel sided posts, which were popular once, lack character. The use of natural timber with all its bumps and kinks and irregularity is becoming popular in its place.

In the chapter, *Engaging with the Ground*, we give guidance about the minimum size the timber should be when installed directly in the ground and, alternatively, suggested methods of installing a round post in a bracket to give support in each direction. We also considered that some applications, those that are free standing, should be considered as if they are an H5 application because of the increase in risk. The chapter, *Timber Specifications*, explained how to achieve an H5 equivalence without reverting to CCA or creosote through using timber with natural durability. Species that are unsuitable for use in Australia for playground construction have been discussed in the Chapter, *Standards and Fitness for Purpose*.

The two main issues that must be attended to in design are splitting heads and longitudinal splitting both of which can produce potential finger entrapments. A third potential finger entrapment can occur through not spacing the logs apart when connecting them.

---

[93] A 200 mm H5 pine post could have a design life of 100 years in SE Queensland!

Splitting Heads

Figure 31. Robinia as delivered to site

Figure 32. The same material after weathering

The heads of some round timbers are prone to splitting, or "star bursting" as it is known in the industry. In Figure 31 and Figure 32 this effect can be seen and had there not been a band at the end the effect would have been far worse. Here we have a low-density material (660-750 kg M3 dry) with higher shrinkage (7.2%), it really cannot do anything else unless a great deal of care is taken. This can affect the item structurally especially when fasteners pass through these splits but is aesthetically poor as the item is not ageing gracefully and will be subject to rot. Very importantly, the risk of splinters and finger entrapment is significant. One supplier says of such splitting:

> "Only on the upper side of horizontal beams with large splits between 8 mm and 25 mm wide is there some risk of this type of entrapment. In over 30 years of trading, [our company] has not heard of an incident of this type of accident on their equipment, despite extensive use of this type of timber. Even with such splits, the equipment is approved to BS EN 1176"[94] [95]

Frankly, we do not understand how it is possible for timber that is split as badly as this could ever meet a standard if we are concerned with fitness for purpose. This is discussed in more depth in the chapter *Inspection and Maintenance*. This brings us to the point of this book, which is not whether timber should meet standards but rather understanding when it is fit for purpose.

---

[94] Richter Spielgerate GmbH. *Splits (shakes) in Timber* (no publication details) 1.
[95] Issued as AS 4685 with Australian variations.

Splitting on low shrinkage species (Maximum 3%)

Pine: It is very unusual for the heads of pine to starburst. Longitudinal splits are likely to occur however, but are generally (but not always) under 8 mm. If the timber is being used in a horizontal alignment the ends do not need to be capped but should simply be monitored. When used vertically it is important that the timber is water shedding with an angled top or otherwise the timber should be capped. In small diameter material it will be virtually all sapwood and easily treated almost all the way through. The treatment should have a water repellent, usually a wax, added.[96]

Cypress: Again, like pine it is unusual for the heads to starburst and head splitting is unusual. It should be detailed in the same way as pine. The heart and heartwood are durable

Hardwood: Species such as brigalow and lancewood have very low shrinkage and will have a durability equal to or even higher than cypress. These should be detailed in the same way as pine.

Splitting on higher shrinkage species (3.1 to 7.5%)

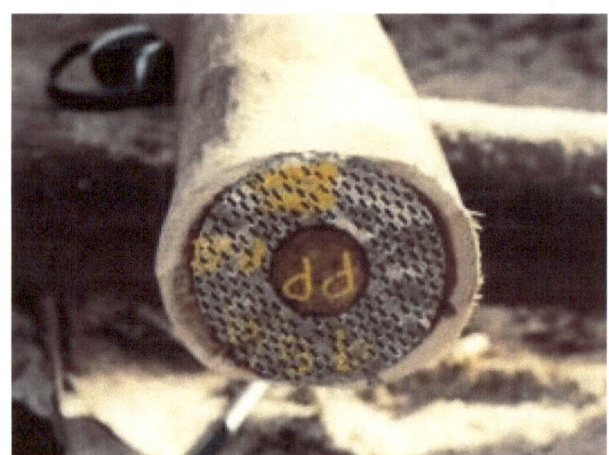 

Figure 33.   Polecat (only use with a cap)   Figure 34.   Cake tins make effective caps

This higher range of shrinkage from 3.1 to 7.5% only applies to hardwood. The higher figure is set to the shrinkage rate of narrow leaved red ironbark. It should be noted that shrinkage can be much higher e.g., turpentine at 13% and timbers with higher rates of shrinkage should be excluded in your specification. From Ted's experience with powerpoles he has observed that once a piece is vertical and the weather affects all "faces" that splitting is less of an issue than with horizontal pieces where one side is baked and the other cool. Notwithstanding, all ends should be restrained and capped whether being used horizontally or vertically. Steel bands as shown in Figure 32 are not satisfactory.[97] Ted suggests using cake tins as the caps! They are available in a range of sizes down to 100 mm. Turned upside down they no longer resemble a cake tin but a very expensive aluminium cap with a neat, rolled edge. Whatever cap you use, it needs to

---

[96] Evans, Philip. *Pers. Com*. December 28, 2020
[97] Ted even experimented with steel bands that had to be pressed on, but these did not work either.

be used in conjunction with a "Polecat", a circular nail plate.[98] Best practice in capping the ends would be:

1. Using a template in conjunction with a router, form an accurate end to the round that suits the appropriate cap.
2. Drive in the appropriately sized "Polecat", grinding off any protruding steel.
3. Seal with copper naphthenate (CN) emulsion
4. Fit the cap over the end, a suitable adhesive also would be appropriate.
5. Secure the cap with stainless steel screws Note: use a nylon washer under the head to prevent corrosion.

Size is critical here and Ted's experience, which is supported by others with a background in the pole industry[99] is that with these higher shrinkage rates, anything that has a head size under 200 mm is likely to split and for this reason should be avoided.

Note: Under no circumstance should a "Polecat" be used without a cap in a playground situation. The constant wetting and drying will force the plate out of the end grain exposing very sharp edges. The plating at capping of the post is aimed at reducing the possibility of having finger entrapment. Best practice would have a 3 mm air space under the cap[100] but this will not stand up to playground activity.

---

[98] This product was developed by Ted to stop the heads of powerpoles splitting when laying horizontally in his pole yard.
[99] Hyne, James. *Pers. Com.* December 9, 2020. "I agree with your assertion that going much smaller than 200mm can be an issue, particularly with spotted gum and species that have broad sap bands. Other species with narrow sap bands such as Ironbark are less prone to splitting in smaller diameters."
[100] Tingley, Dan. *Pers. Com.* April 22, 2021.

Longitudinal Checks

Figure 35. Longitudinal split in pine in a horizontal application

Figure 36. Longitudinal split in pine in a vertical application

Longitudinal splits, termed checks, are very common in pine and while they will mainly be under 8 mm in width, they can at times be so severe that they become a finger entrapment as shown in Figure 35 and Figure 36. Checking can reduce the holding power of fasteners and the strength of the wood. Further, when timber of low durability such as larch or disputed durability such as robinia is used, checks can promote decay by allowing moisture to enter the core of the timber.[101] This is an issue almost unique to pine and there does not appear to be a solution without processing in some way. Excessive checking occurs because the outside, which has swelled during preservation, starts to shrink, while the inside remains the same size as it is losing moisture much more slowly. It was determined that the only way to deal with this as rounds was:

- to drill a hole down the centre and allow the timber to dry from the inside as well as the outside and so reducing the stress on the timber, or
- To make at least two kerfs[102] along the length.

---

[101] Evans, Philip D., Robin Wingate-Hill, Simon C. Barry. 2000. "The Effects of Different Kerfing and Centre-Boring Treatments on the Checking of ACQ Treated Pine Posts Exposed to the Weather." *Forest Products Journal* 50 (2), 59.

[102] A single kerf can open to 10 mm wide during an Australian summer. Philip D. Evans, Robin Wingate-Hill, Simon C. Barry. 1997. "The Ability of Physical Treatments to Reduce Checking in Preservative-treated Slash Pine Posts." *Australian Forest Journal* 47 (5), 55.

Both these options have proven to reduce the number and size of checks in preservative treated pine after a year's exposure.[103] It is not an easy ask to form a hole the full length of a post but such timber in a true diameter round is available in New Zealand at least.[104] Given that it is probably impractical to source hollow core timber in Australia, In Ted's opinion the only practical way of designing out this natural characteristic of pine is through kerfs sawn the full length. This at least controls where the "split" occurs and how large it is. To avoid splinters the edges would need to be arrised. The suggested size of the hole is at least 35 mm and of each kerf 25x3 mm.[105] If no steps are taken to minimise checking is used, then the timber must be monitored and filled with a proprietary flexible non-pick type filler. There is little doubt that the appearance of the timber will be adversely affected.

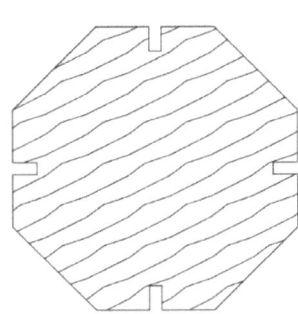

Another method that Ted has seen used with success, at least in the UK is by processing the parallel round further by passing it through a planer and forming it into an octagon where at least 4 sides have shallow kerfs.[106] This is a relatively straightforward machining process but tooling cost would be high so it would only be appropriate for ongoing applications.

Preparing Round Timber

Figure 37. Octagonal post with kerfs

General guidelines for preparing natural round hardwood for playground timber are as follows:[107]

Straightness:	The general guideline is that the line from the centre of the ends must not leave the pole along its length. This is quite possible in a long piece.
limbs:	Each limb is to be planed smooth for appearance and most importantly to enable checking for rot. Where rot is present a spike is driven in to determine its extent. When shallow (approx. 50 mm in a 200 -250 mm diameter), it is to be removed and the patch "veed" out to permit rain to drain away. Unsound knots in the critical area (1 m above and 0.6 m below ground line) are not permitted and the piece must be rejected, or if overlength, cut back.
Lumps:	lumps on the piece are usually associated with overgrown damaged limbs and are to be treated in the same manner as limbs.
Injury:	Where there is a danger of splinters to the contractors for the playground and to children from axe marks the timber must be planed smooth.

---

[103] Evans. *Ability* …, 55.
[104] Refer TTT Products, *Unilog*. URL: https://www.unilog.co.nz/product-7-unilog Date accessed: December 28, 2020
[105] Evans. *Ability* …, 52. Ted achieved the 3 mm cut by removing the kerf from a regular, not tungsten tip, circular saw
[106] Ted saw this product when visiting HLD (formerly Hickson Leisure Decision) a division of John Brash Group at Gainsborough in the UK. It was sold as *Octawood*. The product was patented but it is expected that it would be expired by now.
[107] These guidelines are drawn from the work instructions in the quality program Ted had in place for preparing power poles.

Discolouration: This is found in the centre of knots that often prove faulty. These are to be tested.

Moisture content: The rounds are periodically checked for moisture using an electrical resistance type moisture meter. The moisture content of the sapwood measured at its full depth in the poles should be between 30-40% and preferably at 30-35% before preservation can occur. (This is fibre saturation point with the free moisture released)

Fastening.

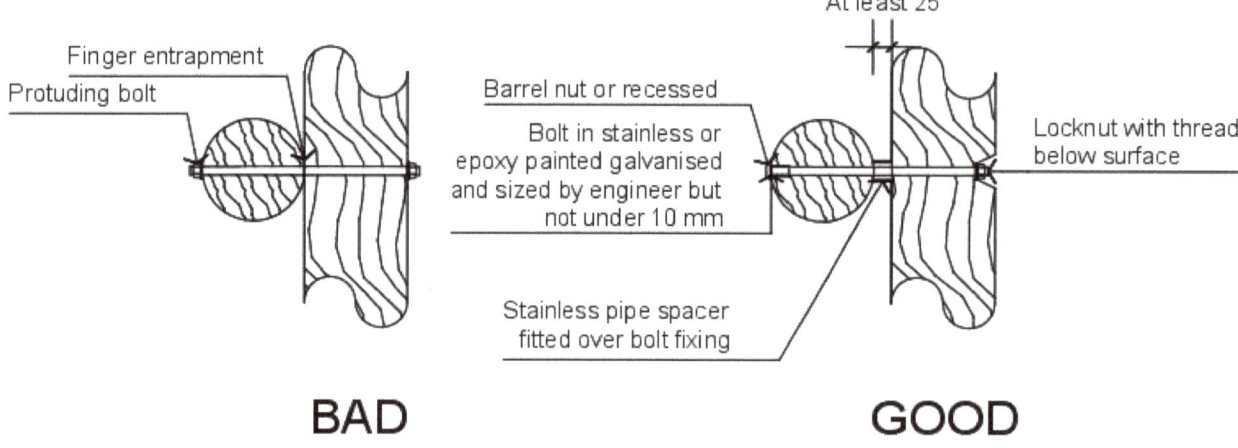

Figure 38. Good and bad practice for joining round timber

The type of fastener recommended will be discussed in the chapter entitled *Fasteners*. There is a consideration that needs dealing within this chapter, namely avoiding finger entrapment. If two round timbers are simply bolted together as shown in Figure 38 there is a potential for finger entrapment, and they should be spaced a minimum of 25 mm apart. Proprietary spacers are available in Europe to suit a range of different diameters but it could be questioned whether they will have the necessary UV protection to last 30 years in our extreme climate. Ralph simply uses a cut stainless pipe as spacers which will be easier to source in Australia and will never need replacing.

Critical Zone

Figure 39. Powerpole marked up with information to permit quick grading for quality and size.

The Standard for powerpoles *AS3818.11-2009, Timber-Heavy structural products-Visually graded part 11:P Utility poles* recognises a critical zone for decay and impact which for hardwood is 600 mm below ground line and 1.0 m above and this needs to be virtually clear wood. This needs to be addressed firstly in the specification and then by an inspection prior to installation. When producing powerpoles, Ted had his staff mark the critical zone (Figure 39) on the pole for easy identification. This image also shows the basic information needed for quick grading. He did this with permanent timber markers, but a lumber crayon would be appropriate for playgrounds as this breaks down quickly as they are only wax.

Seats and Steppers

The main concern with round seats and steppers is how to engage with the ground so as to minimise maintenance and that is dealt with in that chapter. It is sufficient to note here that the sapwood should either be removed or treated. Ted's experience is that the stepper needs to be a minimum of 150 mm thick and ideally 200 mm so as not to break into segments.

4 SPECIAL CONSIDERATIONS WITH CCA

How Dangerous is CCA?

Figure 40.   CCA treated pine playground with embedded posts and made from natural tapering posts is still sound after 32 years (pine was painted at some stage)

The use of CCA in playgrounds has been banned by the APVMA in Australia since 2005 but, because it works so well there would still be a significant amount of CCA treated infrastructure in place. Also, playground designers are unknowingly, asking for CCA when they insist on H5 which, in practice, is only available in CCA. While the western world has largely turned its back on CCA, worldwide it is still the most common preservative.[108] Is the widespread use of CCA then just a matter of third world poverty, taking the less expensive option without due regard to the health of users? Or is it a reasonable response to the evidence? When the APVMA reviewed the scientific studies into CCA, which probably range into the multi thousand, it concluded:

> "Based on a consideration of the exposure to CCA treated timber products, in particular children's play equipment, there was no compelling evidence from the available data to conclude that there was likely to be an unacceptable risk to public health from arsenic from CCA treated timber."[109]

---

[108] Jensen. Greg. *Pers. Com.* Feb 12, 2012.
[109] APVMA. *The Reconsideration of Registrations of Arsenic Timber Treatment Products (CCA and arsenic trioxide) and*

Further, The Western Australian Government website quantified the actual risk from CCA contact from a playground saying by saying:

> "Children who place their hands in their mouth after playing on CCA treated wooden playground equipment do increase their risk of arsenic exposure. International research has found, however, that it:
>
> - only contributes between 2–8 per cent of the safe daily acceptable limits set by the World Health Organisation, and
> - is within the safe daily acceptable limits set by the Australian Department of Health and Ageing.
>
> This combined arsenic exposure is still less than a third of the amount that a child can be exposed to in their lifetime before it significantly affects their health. Small amounts of arsenic are also commonly found in the environment, our food and drinking water."[110]

The conclusion reached by the APVMA, in face of this less than overwhelming evidence, was "Evidence of health problems associated with this use has not been proven. Because arsenic at higher levels is a carcinogen, and alternative wood preservatives are available, restrictions in some domestic applications will occur as a precaution."[111]

CCA was removed from segments of the Australian market, not because it was proven dangerous but because it was not proven safe. Unfortunately, industry sources told Ted the APVMA could not agree with the industry on the format of test regime whereby it may be proven to be safe. The New Zealand Authorities reviewed the same data and came to a different conclusion. Their report said "CCA-treated wood has also been in use for many years without discernible health effects suggesting that if there is a true increased risk it is very small".[112] The New Zealanders attempted to quantify the risk in that country. They maintain that an increased risk of one in 100,000 over a 70-year lifetime from exposure to a carcinogen was acceptable.[113] The actual risk is far less than this.[114] Bear in mind that the very visit to a playground is probably more dangerous. There are said to be in the order of 250,000 playground injuries in Australia each year, these are real injuries and should put the unproven risk of CCA into perspective![115]

The New Zealand study makes the observation "Despite uncertainty and potential overestimation of

---

Their Associated Labels - Report of Review Findings and Regulatory Outcomes Final Report Part 1 - Toxicological Assessment (Canberra, 2005) 19. URL: https://apvma.gov.au/sites/default/files/publication/14316-arsenic-summary.pdf Date accessed: December 7, 2020.

[110] Government of Western Australia, Department of Health. *Stay safe around copper chrome arsenate treated wood.* HTTP: https://www.healthywa.wa.gov.au/Articles/S_T/Stay-safe-around-copper-chrome-arsenate-treated-woodarsenate treated wood Date accessed: December 7, 2020

[111] CSIRO. *The Facts About CCA Treated Timber* Page 7. http://www.csiro.au/en/Outcomes/Food-and-Agriculture/CCATreatedTimber/CCA-safety-overview.aspx Date accessed, 21 April 2012.

[112] Read, Deborah. *Report on Copper Chrome and Arsenic Treated Timber.* ERMANZ April 2003 https://www.epa.govt.nz/assets/Uploads/Documents/Hazardous-Substances/Guidance/Report-on-CCA-safety-by-Deborah-Read-April-2003.pdf Date accessed, 14 February 2021, 57.

[113] Read. *Report...*, 57.

[114] Read. *Report...*, 56-9.

[115] This figure was mentioned at a Kidsafe conference Ted spoke at in around 2011. Kidsafe Victoria give actual hospitalisations from playground injuries at 6000 per year or roughly 10% of all children's admissions. Kidsafe Victoria, *Action to Reduce Playground Injuries*, http://www.kidsafevic.com.au/news/25-action-to-reduce-playground-injuries. Date accessed 28 May 2012. Estimates of the number of injuries vary greatly. Ted has seen figures quoted varying between 100,000 to 500,000!

cancer risk it would be prudent public health policy to reduce human exposure to arsenic from all sources wherever feasible".[116] Yet the implications of this statement are enormous. When Ted tested his employees, who worked in his timber treatment plant for arsenic levels it was essential that they did not drink beer or eat seafood for three days beforehand! If they did eat or drink these common items, they could give a false high reading because of their arsenic content. Wouldn't consistency also require that these also be banned?

But facts are worth very little when dealing with grandmothers who grew up with *Arsenic and Old Lace* and young mothers who saw the fictional account of CCA poisoning in *The Practice*. There are alternatives available to counter these perceptions and it is simply much easier to use them than to fight against the tide. While theoretically there are alternatives to CCA available for most applications, it is not simply a matter of specifying Tanalith E treated to H5 instead of CCA treated to H5 (which in many cases was over-specification). Because of the much higher chemical cost and the availability of plants licensed to treat to the higher levels, these alternative treatments will probably not be realisable. As mentioned earlier, they simply never were achievable in sawn timber.

It is necessary to take care when specifying any timber treatments for any application, not just playgrounds to ensure you do not put yourself in a situation that may require future remedial action or client complaints. CCA is still legal for some products such as commercial decking (but illegal for domestic) but may still be rejected by the client.[117]

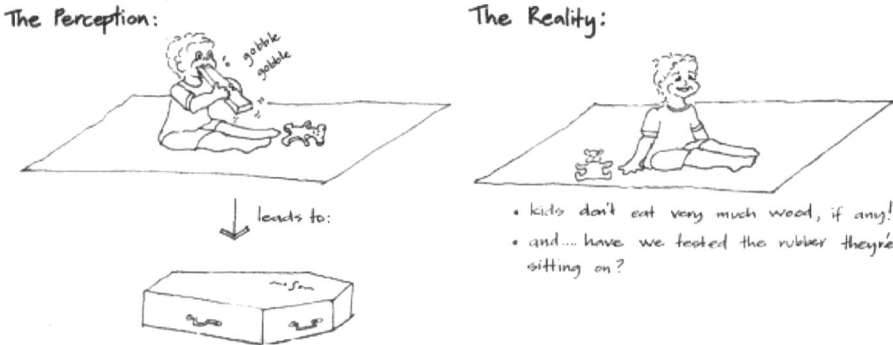

Figure 41.   A cartoon by Fiona Robbe.

A few years ago, Ted spoke at a timber treaters' conference and while there met with a representative of the APVMA. He asked, "Have all the products that are used in children's playgrounds been subject to the same scrutiny as CCA." The reply was "I hope so." The fact is they have not been. This was confirmed 12 months later when Ted spoke at a Kidsafe conference on the subject of treating timber. During lunch he sat near two manufacturers of rubber soft fall and they were expressing concern about the safety of their product. It is doubtful that it has been studied in anywhere near the same extent as CCA.[118] The likely scenario is that when all the products that we use in children's playground have been

---

[116] Read. *Report…*, 62.

[117] A guide to acceptable use is available at http://www.outdoorstructures.com.au/pdf/cca_acceptable_usage.pdf. Not every application is covered in this list, e.g., bollards.

[118] An internet search shows that this is a much-debated subject. See Huber, Rolf. *Health Effects of Tire Rubber Exposure*. URL: https://playgroundprofessionals.com/surfaces/rubber/health-effects-tire-rubber-exposure Date Accessed: 7 December 2020. Smith, A.H. Duggan, H.M. Wright C "Assessment of cancer clusters using limited cohort data with spreadsheets: application to a leukaemia cluster among rubber workers," *American Journal of Industrial Medicine*, 1994 Jun;25(6):813-23 may be relevant.

subject to the same scrutiny as CCA there is likely to be nothing left to design with!

What Can be Done with Existing CCA Infrastructure?

Figure 42.   Leaching Trials.   Figure 43.   Contact Trials.

If asset owners are not prepared to maintain their structures, they should pull them out immediately, whether they are made of steel or timber, untreated or treated. Surely the danger from a loose bolt is more real (and likely) than a possible risk from a treatment or a particular material, e.g., paint or softfall? Wise asset management dictates that timber infrastructure should be regularly maintained with a simple, effective maintenance program, regardless of the treatment employed. This maintenance program should include the simplest preparation and re-application techniques. Preparation should be able to be performed quickly by unskilled labour. The product best fitting this description is penetrating oil.

The APVMA has no regulatory authority over existing structures constructed of CCA treated timber and so has made no recommendation with respect to future action for existing structures. CCA treated timber which is processed in Australia is now illegal for many new traditional applications. Serious concern (and almost panic) has been expressed in many quarters about what to do with existing CCA structures. Understandably asset owners simply did not know what to do with existing CCA treated infrastructure. While the APVMA did not require existing CCA timber to be removed even from children's playgrounds and their ruling gave no clear guidance as to what to do with it, sealing the timber with a penetrating oil was suggested as a potential effective solution. They said:

> "Information is limited on the possible benefits of painting treated-timber (including existing structures) to reduce possible risks. Some scientific studies indicate that certain penetrating coatings, such as oil-based semi-transparent stains, when used on a regular basis ***may***[119] reduce the potential for CCA exposure. However, there have been some questions raised about the effectiveness of film-forming or non-penetrating stains because of cracking, peeling and flaking".[120]

This suggestion is exactly the same as wise asset management. However, the APVMA says MAY reduce exposure. Does it in actual fact work?

When trading as Outdoor Structures Australia, Ted asked Arch Chemicals who manufacture Tanacoat

---

[119] Underlining and bold added by author.
[120] APVMA, *Reconsideration …*, 15.

(initially exclusively for his business) to undertake testing to determine if this sealing does in fact happen. Tanacoat has been proven to be remarkably effective in sealing CCA treated timber. Under laboratory simulation, (Figure 42 and Figure 43) leaching of the active constituents was reduced by 50% and transfer by physical contact to virtually one twentieth.[121] So, applying Tanacoat to timber allows the asset owner to maintain good timber maintenance practices and deal with CCA at the same time.[122]

For Ted, the imponderable is why APVMA would promote penetrating oils which must be applied at least annually over paint that can have a multiyear life. Ted put this question to treatment chemical suppliers, and no one could provide the answer, but it was suggested that it may be simply a question of not trusting that the paint would be maintained. Ralph points out that paint is more dependable on steel than timber as there is less movement of the substrate steel. In a playground setting however, people want to see that the structure is timber so a clear coating is favoured over an opaque painted finish. This is discussed further on the chapter *Inspection and Maintenance* where penetrating oils are favoured over film finishes.

CCA Treatment and Fire

A long time ago Ted installed new cattle fencing in some timber land the family owned at the time. He used split hardwood posts which are the normal posts used in that location. As the posts contained sapwood, which was going to decay, Ted thought it would be wise and treat the posts with CCA. The logic was hard to fault at the time, but the end result was the opposite of what we intended. When the first fire came through, normally not much of an issue, we lost most of the posts which burned completely to the ground. Ted learnt very quickly that there can be a major issue with CCA treatment and fire. The same is equally true of CCA treated playground timber which may be subject to vandalism through fire, but this can be very effectively dealt with by using intumescent paint on the posts. Ralph believes that if the site is assessed as having a potential arson risk it is better to use steel posts as the cost of intumescent paint is considerable.

Avoiding CCA in design and specification

An H5 product is what is needed for a free-standing embedded post. It is possible to avoid CCA but not once a playground designer has written H5! Basically, a playground designer must incorporate a "work around" which will achieve the desired end result by relying on natural durability and best practice in engaging with the ground. The chapter on timber specification gave guidance on how to specify to avoid this chemical and the chapter, *Engaging with the Ground* explains how to detail a post. Those chapters stress that common practice is often bad practice. Basically, it involves using a durability Class 1 in-ground hardwood post with either no or minimal sapwood if sawn or, for a natural round, the sapwood treated to H3. Measurements of the post are to be taken under sap. A species with a narrow sapwood band should be used such as ironbark as opposed to tallowwood.[123] The post must not be set in concrete or even no fines concrete. An example of this work around can be seen in Case History 1, Playground on the Broadwater, Southport, Queensland.

---

[121] Detailed results are found at https://www.outdoorstructures.com.au/pdf/cca_timber_treatment_analysis.pdf and the methodology used is found at
https://www.outdoorstructures.com.au/pdf/cca_timber_treatment_methodology.pdf

[122] Further information on sealing CCA can be found on the USEPA website:
http://www.epa.gov/scipoly/sap/meetings/2006/november/november2006finalmeetingminutes.pdf.

[123] Sapwood on ironbark can be up to 20 mm wide but is typically closer to 12 mm. sapwood on tallowwood will invariably almost twice that of ironbark.

5 TIMBER SPECIFICATIONS

Considerations When Specifying Playground Timber

In the chapters dealing with sawn and round timber, Ted presented his basis for the specifications that are provided in this chapter and the following is basically a summary of what has preceded. Not all applications present the same risk. The following specification makes a distinction between freestanding structures by which we mean one that can fall over if decay occurs at the groundline e.g., a two-post swing and one that has multiple opposed posts that cannot fall e.g., a four-post swing.

Figure 44. Free standing timber post swing

Figure 45. Timber post swing that is self-supporting.

Hardwood-Sawn

Hardwood sawn-above-ground

Hardwood shall be durability Class 1 above-ground from the following species (specifier to nominate). The timber is to be supplied visually graded to the requirements of Structural Grade 1 to *AS2082 Timber—Hardwood—Visually stress-graded for structural purposes*. There is an extra requirement that tight or loose gum veins that join at an edge are not permitted unless out of reach of children. Sapwood is to be treated to H3 (excluding CCA, creosote or LOSP) to *AS1604.1 Specification for preservative treatment Sawn and round timber*. Included heart is only permitted in sizes where the smallest dimension is 175 mm or larger. Timber with included heart shall have arrised expansion grooves as detailed (specifier to nominate where and size) and the heart shall be approximately central. The timber shall be (specifier to nominate rough sawn, rough sawn sanded, or dressed), pencil rounded with a (specifier to nominate) mm radius.

Note 1: Rough sawn hardwood absorbs the oil finishes better than dressed hardwood.
Note 2: Ensure you do not have a conflicting F grade mentioned. Wording like "Calculations are based on F(insert). The physical propertied described will meet or most likely exceed this F grade. Timber is to be supplied to the physical properties".
Note 3: What will you say about independent verification of grade?

Note 4: Consider using the standard trade name in conjunction with the botanical names of all species associated with that name to avoid substitution by a product with a similar local or marketing name.

Hardwood sawn - in-ground

Hardwood shall be durability Class 1 in-ground from the following species (specifier to nominate). The timer is to be supplied visually graded to the requirements of Structural Grade 1 to AS2082 *Timber—Hardwood—Visually stress-graded for structural purposes*. There is an extra requirement that tight or loose gum veins that join at an edge are not permitted unless buried or out of reach of children. Sapwood, which is not to exceed 20% of the cross section is to be treated to H3[124] (excluding CCA Creosote or LOSP) to *AS1604.1 Specification for preservative treatment Sawn and round timber*. Included heart is only permitted in sizes the smallest dimension is 175 mm or larger. Timber with included heart shall have arrised expansion grooves as detailed (specifier to nominate where) and the heart shall be approximately central. The timber shall be (specifier to nominate rough sawn, rough sawn sanded, or dressed), pencil rounded with a (specifier to nominate) mm radius.

Note 1: Refer to the chapter, *Engaging with the Ground* for minimum timber size and construction practice.
Note 2: Rough sawn hardwood absorbs the oil finishes better than dressed hardwood.
Note 3: Ensure you do not have a conflicting F grade mentioned. Wording like "Calculations are based on F(insert). The physical propertied described will meet or most likely exceed this F grade. Timber is to be supplied to the physical properties".
Note 4: What will you say about independent verification of grade?
Note 5: Consider using the standard trade name in conjunction with the botanical names of all species associated with that name to avoid substitution by a product with a similar local or marketing name.

Hardwood kiln dried decking

Kiln dried hardwood decking shall be select grade to *AS2796.2 Timber—Hardwood—Sawn and milled products Part 2: Grade description* from the following species (specifier to nominate). The sides shall be square, and the top surface shall be (specifier to nominate if the timber is dressed or rough sawn and whether the addition of wire buffed is required on sawn finish [125]), There is the additional requirement that timber is not permitted where two loose gum veins join at a corner. Sapwood shall be treated to Level H3 (excluding CCA or Creosote or LOSP) to *AS1604.1 Specification for preservative treatment Sawn and round timber*.

Figure 46. Taper sided decking can possibly be a finger entrapment

Note 1: Rough sawn hardwood absorbs the oil finishes better than dressed hardwood and has the needed slip resistance especially if the deck is wet.

---

[124] H3 is correct. The high natural durability with low sapwood content will achieve the same outcome as H5 (or probably better).
[125] While dressed finish is going to be more readily available, Ted and Ralph do not recommend it unless under cover.

Note 2: Ensure you do not have a conflicting F grade mentioned. Wording like "Calculations are based on F(insert). The physical propertied described will meet or most likely exceed this F grade. Timber is to be supplied to the physical properties".
Note 3: What will you say about independent verification of grade?
Note 4: Consider using the standard trade name in conjunction with the botanical names of all species associated with that name to avoid substitution by a product with a similar local or marketing name.

Hardwood Unseasoned decking

Hardwood decking 35 mm and above where specified may be supplied unseasoned to the following specification. Timber shall be selected from the following species, spotted gum, tallowwood, ironbark.[126] The top surface will be lightly sanded. At the time of grading, the bottom and sides of the plank shall conform to AS2082 *Timber—Hardwood—Visually stress-graded for structural purposes*, Structural Grade 2 while the exposed surface shall conform to the following.[127] The sides are to be square, not tapered.

Freedom from the following on the rough sawn (upper) face-

Loose & unsound knots	Shakes
Loose Gum Veins	Knot holes
Termite Galleries	Want, wane & bark
Checks wider than 1 mm	End splits wider than 1 mm
Included bark	Borer holes larger than 3 mm

In addition, permitted defects shall not cover more than 15% of the top face.

Permissible defects on the upper face may include 1 only borer hole up to 6mm dia. per plank.

Preservative Treatment, Treatment, natural durability classes and combinations shall conform to *AS1604.1 Specification for preservative treatment Sawn and round timber*. Sapwood shall be treated to Level H3 without CCA or Creosote or LOSP.

Note 1: Ensure you have given detailed laying instructions as you must accommodate the shrinkage in unseasoned decking. See the chapter *Design Details*.
Note 2: Ensure you do not have a conflicting F grade mentioned. Wording like "Calculations are based on F(insert). The physical propertied described will meet or most likely exceed this F grade. Timber is to be supplied to the physical properties".
Note 3: What will you say about independent verification of grade?
Note 4: Consider using the standard trade name in conjunction with the botanical names of all species associated with that name to avoid substitution by a product with a similar local or marketing name.

Cypress Sawn

---

[126] Extreme care should be exercised when deviating from these three. Many species offered such as blackbutt, in Ted's opinion are inferior.

[127] This specification follows the requirements of Ted's Deckwood which has proven to provide excellent service.

Cypress-sawn all applications except decking
Cypress shall be supplied visually graded to F7 to the requirements of *AS2858 Timber—Softwood—Visually stressgraded for structural purposes.* Sapwood content shall be 10% maximum. The timber shall be (specifier to nominate if the timber is dressed or rough sawn and whether the addition of wire buffed is required on sawn finish [128]), pencil rounded (specifier to nominate if the addition of wire buffed of sawn finish is required).

Note 1: Refer to the chapter, *Engaging with the Ground* for minimum timber size and construction practice.
Note 2: What will you say about independent verification of grade?

Cypress-sawn decking
As the sapwood cannot be treated, we do not recommend cypress for weather exposed decking.

Plantation Pine Sawn

Pine - General
It should be noted that pine is inferior to both hardwood and cypress when it comes to playground timber. It requires specification far beyond the normal structural standards to ensure it is successful. It is very doubtful whether the timber specifications we give can be met. Given the small volumes that will be involved most suppliers will not be prepared to do what is necessary to produce what is needed but the specifier should not contemplate a lesser standard.

Plantation pine - above-ground - sawn
Structural Grade 1 to *AS2858 Timber—Softwood—Visually stressgraded for structural purposes* or MGP15 if visual grading is not available, treated to H3 (not CCA, creosote or LOSP) to *AS1604.1 Specification for preservative treatment Sawn and round timber.* The maximum heartwood content is 10% unless incised to a depth of 8 mm for 45 mm thick (5 mm for 35 mm).

Plantation pine - above-ground – decking
We do not recommend pine decking for weather exposed applications as it is prone to warp and splinter.

Plantation pine - In-ground – Sawn, self-supporting
Structural Grade 1 to *AS2858 Timber—Softwood—Visually stressgraded for structural purposes* or MGP15 if visual grading is not available, treated to H4 (not CCA or creosote) to *AS1604.1 Specification for preservative treatment Sawn and round timber.* The maximum heartwood content is 10% unless incised to a depth of 10 mm.

Note 1: Refer to the chapter, *Engaging with the Ground* for minimum timber size and construction practice
Note 2: If the timber is to be supplied visually graded, ensure you do not have a conflicting F grade mentioned. Wording like "Calculations are based on F(insert). The physical propertied described will meet

---

[128] Both dressed and rough sawn cypress are readily available but rough sawn will weather and absorb oil better.

or most likely exceed this F grade. Timber is to be supplied to the physical properties".
Note 3: What will you say about independent verification of grade?

Plantation pine - In-ground – sawn free standing
Structural Grade 1 AS2858 Timber—Softwood—Visually stressgraded for structural purposes or MGP15, treated to H5 (not CCA or creosote), maximum heartwood content is 10% unless incised to a depth of 20 mm.

Note 1: Refer to the chapter, *Engaging with the Ground* for minimum timber size and construction practice (Note also that while it is theoretically possible, it is not going to possible to receive timber to this specification due to the small volumes involved)

Note 2: If the timber is to be supplied visually graded, ensure you do not have a conflicting F grade mentioned. Wording like "Calculations are based on F(insert). The physical propertied described will meet or most likely exceed this F grade. Timber is to be supplied to the physical properties".

Hardwood Natural Rounds

Hardwood, natural round - In-ground – self supporting[129]
Natural round hardwood intended for in-ground use in a self-supporting item shall be durability Class 1 in-ground from the following species (specifier to nominate) and treated to H4 (without CCA or creosote). The timber shall be from essentially sound wood, free of live insect attack and with sufficient straightness such that a line drawn from the centre of each end does not leave the timber. The following imperfections are permitted except in the critical zone being 1.0 m above groundline and 600 mm below.

- Surface rot pockets (maximum of two) are to be shallow and are not in aggregate to exceed 10% of the circumference in any 600 mm length and are to be cleared for drainage
- Insect holes are not to be clustered in a way that impact the strength of the sapwood
- Grub holes up to 30 mm in diameter and to be more than a metre apart. Holes in excess of 8 mm[130] must be filled with a non-pick filler
- Gum pockets not exceeding 20 mm deep
- Unsound knots not to exceed 5% of the circumference
- Sound knots not to exceed 20% of the circumference in any 600 mm
- Axe marks across the grain and other mechanical damage to be removed
- Pipe[131] maximum 20% of cross section area
- End splits providing the timber is sufficiently overlength so they will be removed prior to fitting of end caps, and

---

[129] This specification is drawn largely from AS 3818.11-2009, *Timber-Heavy structural products-Visually graded part 11:P Utility poles*, Section 1 and 3 but incorporates some of Ted's experience, e.g., gum pockets.

[130] One playground certifier recommends filling the cracks when it reaches 5 mm rather than waiting till it reaches 8 mm. Consulting Coordination Australia. *Timber Splitting and Cracking Rectification. Version 1.* (Sydney: Consulting Coordination Australia .2018) 1.

[131] Pipe is a trade term for a hole up the centre. The hole in the centre of a *Polecat* (Figure 33) is to allow for inspection of the centre. This product was developed by Ted.

- Dry side is not to be more than 20% of the circumference and can be placed either down or vertical.

Note 1: H4 is available but not as readily available as H3 and the higher level of treatment is not always achieved. You can substitute durability Class 1 in-ground treated to H3 and dimension is to be measured under the sapwood. Everything else remains the same

Note 2: Consider using the standard trade name in conjunction with the botanical names of all species associated with that name to avoid substitution by a product with a similar local or marketing name.

Hardwood, natural round - In-ground - free standing

The specification will be the same as for self-supporting above except that it is critical that durability Class 1 in-ground timber is used in conjunction with treatment to H5 without CCA or creosote.

Note: As this will not be available the alternate specification used for self-supporting, i.e., durability Class 1 in-ground with treatment to H3 and measurement taken under the sapwood will give equal performance to H5 treatment.

Note 2: Consider using the standard trade name in conjunction with the botanical names of all species associated with that name to avoid substitution by a product with a similar local or marketing name

Cypress Natural Rounds

Cypress natural round - In-ground self-supporting[132]

Natural round cypress intended for in-ground use with free standing playgrounds shall have the sapwood substantially removed. Any nominated diameter is under sapwood. The timber shall be from essentially sound wood, free of live insect attack and unsound knots and with sufficient straightness such that a line drawn from the centre of each end does not leave the timber. The following imperfections to a limit of two per 600 mm are permitted except in the critical zone being 1.0 m above groundline and 600 mm below.

- Surface rot pockets are to be shallow and not in aggregate to exceed 10% of the circumference in a 600mm length and are to be cleared for drainage
- Insect holes are not to be clustered in a way that impact the strength of the sapwood
- Resin pockets scattered and not exceeding 10% of the circumference
- Sound knots in aggregate not to exceed 20% of the circumference in any 300 mm (single knot not to exceed 10%)
- Axe marks across the grain and other mechanical damage to be removed
- End splits permitted providing the timber is sufficiently overlength so they will be removed prior to fitting of end caps, and
- Dry side is not to be more than 20% of the circumference and can be placed either down or vertical.

---

[132] This specification is drawn largely from AS 3818.11, *Timber-Heavy structural products-Visually graded, Part 11: Utility poles,* Section 1 and 4. While the specification is intended for plantation pine it should be satisfactory for cypress as well.

Cypress natural round - In-ground free standing

Even though cypress is a high durability Class 2, it is a 2 nonetheless and the sapwood cannot be treated successfully. We do not generally recommended cypress for this application.

Pine Natural Rounds

Pine – natural round – above-ground[133]

Natural round plantation pine, not parallel sided, intended for in-ground use in a self-supporting item shall be from the following species (specifier to nominate) and treated to H3 (without CCA, creosote or LOSP). The timber shall be from essentially sound wood, free of live insect attack and unsound knots and with sufficient straightness such that a line drawn from the centre of each end does not leave the timber. The following imperfections to a limit of two per 600mm are permitted There is no critical zone.

- Surface rot pockets are to be shallow and not in aggregate to exceed 10% of the circumference in a 600 mm length and are to be cleared for drainage
- Insect holes are not to be clustered in a way that impact the strength of the sapwood
- Resin pockets scattered and not exceeding 20 mm deep
- Sound knots not to exceed 20% of the circumference in any 300 mm
- Axe marks across the grain and other mechanical damage to be removed
- End splits providing the timber is sufficiently overlength so they will be removed prior to fitting of end caps, and
- Dry side is not to be more than 20% of the circumference and cab be placed either down or vertical.

Pine – natural round – in-ground self-supporting[134]

Natural round plantation pine, not parallel sided, intended for in-ground use in a self-supporting item shall be from the following species (specifier to nominate) and treated to H4 (without CCA, creosote). The timber shall be from essentially sound wood, free of live insect attack and unsound knots and with sufficient straightness such that a line drawn from the centre of each end does not leave the timber. The following imperfections to a limit of two per 600mm are permitted except in the critical zone being 1.0m above groundline and 600 mm below.

- Surface rot pockets are to be shallow and not in aggregate to exceed 10% of the circumference in a 600 mm length and are to be cleared for drainage
- Insect holes are not to be clustered in a way that impact the strength of the sapwood
- Resin pockets scattered and not exceeding 20 mm deep
- Sound knots not to exceed 20% of the circumference in any 300 mm
- Axe marks across the grain and other mechanical damage to be removed
- End splits providing the timber is sufficiently overlength so they will be removed prior to fitting of end caps, and
- Dry side is not to be more than 20% of the circumference and can be placed either down or vertical.

---

[133] This specification is drawn largely from AS 2209-1994, *Timber-Poles for overhead lines*, Section 1 and 4 with some modification drawn from Ted's experience. It also allows for a lighter treatment and there is no critical zone.

[134] This specification is drawn largely from AS 2209-1994, Timber-Poles for overhead lines, Section 1 and 4.

Pine – natural round – in-ground free standing

The specification will be the same as for self-supporting above except that it is critical that the treatment to H5 without CCA or creosote. It is unlikely that this will be available.

6 ENGAGING WITH THE GROUND

introduction

The structural integrity and longevity of timber playground elements is, in in large part, driven by the connection of the element to the ground. Many components of a timber playground can be maintained simply by replacing them with another piece of timber, however this cannot be said of the support posts. Should there be decay or corrosion, and at groundline is where it would be expected, the whole item may need to be demolished. This is where inspection for decay and termites is critical as there is a very real risk that items can fall over and injure children. Considerable attention must be given on how to engage with the ground to achieve an intended design life.

Embedded Posts

From the outset we wish to make clear that *our recommendation is to set all sawn timber posts, and almost all round posts, in steel supports*! The exception for round posts would be when they meet or exceed the very substantial sizes required under CTIQ. There may be considerable resistance to this in some quarters as it is comparatively inexpensive to simply embed a post, (and there will likely be similar resistance also to providing a suitable post support)!

Figure 47.   Excavation needed to inspect and repair a post in concrete

Figure 48.   Repair to rubber softfall after inspecting and repairing the post

The opposition that we mentioned that a designer will face will be compounded by the real sizes required for in-ground posts that are needed to achieve a minimal maintenance playground. The required large size will add cost, may not even be available and if available, will be very heavy. Of course, appropriate custom-made post bases will involve significant expense also. Notwithstanding, should the asset owner be determined to accept embedded timber posts, what follows is what is necessary to make the post succeed. At the time of writing, much of the Australian fabricated timber playground industry is centred around 125x125 white cypress which is simply too small to guarantee a long life when embedded directly in ground or in concrete. Adding to the argument for the use of metal post supports instead of timber embedment is the cost and difficulty of inspecting (Figure 47). Further, when excavating the soil around a post installed in rubber softfall to allow for inspection, the surface then needs to be repaired. The expected cost in 2020 in Brisbane was $400.[135] Non-destructive test techniques[136] will avoid the cost of a repair if the post proved sound but does nothing to extend the life.

AS 4685 sets the minimum expected design life of playground equipment at 10 years, but most councils and playground providers informally expect a longer life with an expectation of 20 to even 30 years. One Brisbane based playground inspector advised that decay in sawn embedded white cypress posts occurs as early as only 8 years while other posts would reach 15 years.[137] The best performance was only half of what is considered ideal and the worst not reaching the ten-year design life. As Figure 47 and Figure 48 show, undersized posts installed contrary to best practice are not a cheap option for the asset owner. Not all timber elements in a playground would be classified as "equipment" (e.g., a deck[138]) however the same 20–30-year lifespan is a reasonable expectation.[139]

Any embedded post can have its life extended by having a pole bandage applied at installation and this is discussed under the section *Pole bandages* below.

The Importance of Site Location
We are not aware of any playground specific documents that deal with engagement with the ground, so it is necessary to look at the provisions that apply to Class 1 (residential housing) and Class 10 buildings. When it comes to these categories of structure, *Construction Timbers in Queensland, Volumes 1 and 2* is an authoritative source of information on whether a particular timber is suitable for use as embedded posts to achieve a 15- or 50-year design life and also how large the member has to be. Designers and Engineers should be referring to this guide when determining a minimum post size. It uses a four-zone system (Figure 49) taken from *Timber service life design, Design guide for durability* published by Forest and Wood Products Australia. Queensland has all four zones. While CTIQ is the **Law** in Queensland, the zones are applicable nationwide hence the books have nationwide application. As such, both publications are probably the only go-to source for any playground designer seeking to do due diligence in detailing embedded timber.

---

[135] Powell, Brett. *Pers. Com.* 2 March 2021
[136] One option is the EPHOD system utilised by Wood Research and Development Australia and is available Australia wide
[137] Powell, Brett. *Pers. Com.* 2 March 2021.
[138] Decking can be part of a bridge or a cubby which would make it "equipment." Ralph believes all decking should be treated as if it were equipment regardless of where it is situated in the playground.
[139] Fiona Robbe. *Pers. Com.* 21 January 2021.

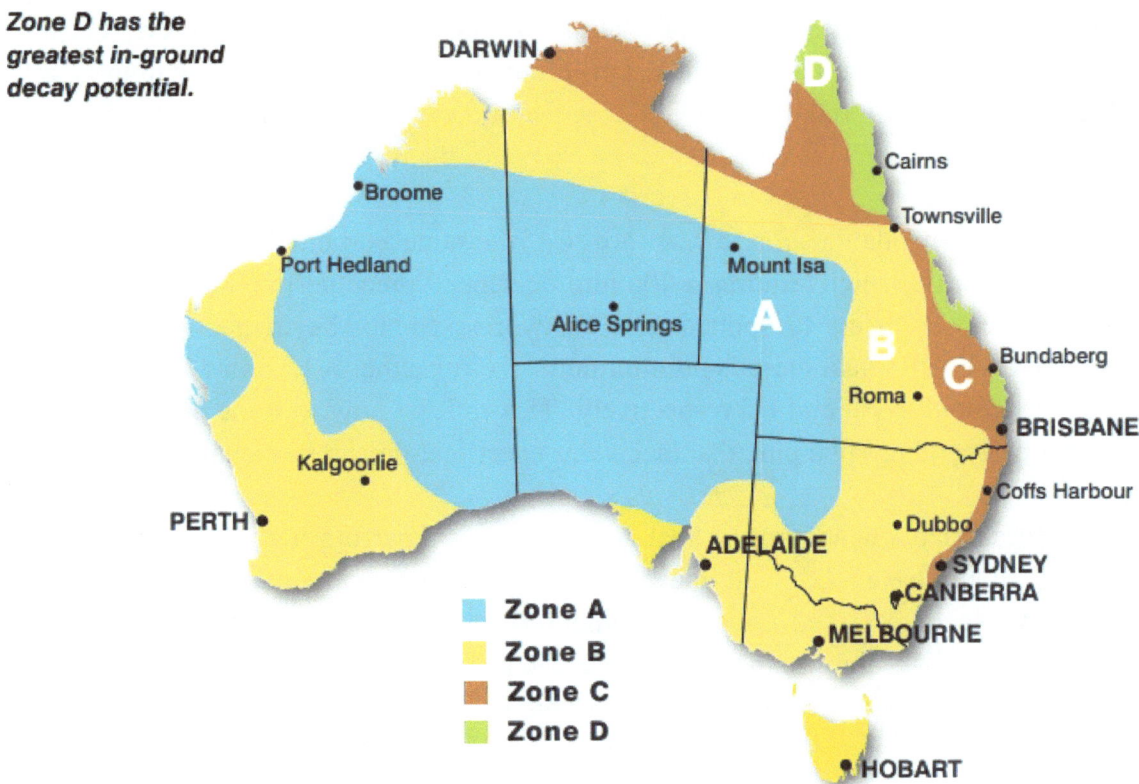

Figure 49.   In-ground hazard zones[140]

But should this excellent guide be used without modification when applied to playgrounds? We consider the application in a playground to be different from that in a home in that the moisture content at groundline is likely to be higher in a playground. This is due to the addition of material such as bark chips, rubber or EPDM softfall above the natural earth and right up to the post. The under surfacing has the potential to retain moisture and in so doing promote decay at a rate above that which is expected in Zones A to C. By contrast, Zone D in normal construction is likely to be constantly moist at ground line. This means that it is probably necessary to make an adjustment to the Zone advice when designing timber structures in a playground situation. Sydney and Brisbane are Zone C, just short of the highest risk while Melbourne, Adelaide and Perth are Zone B, two zones from the highest risk rating. We consider it prudent to treat all free-standing applications as if they were Zone D due to the potential serious consequences of a failure. Where there is no chance of an actual collapse, say in an item with opposing posts, it is probably reasonable just to follow the Zone recommendation. When there is a mixture of freestanding and self-supporting equipment, having two different post details would complicate matters unnecessarily.

Embedded Timber Sizes
Using *Construction Timbers in Queensland* as the guide, a free standing embedded spotted gum post (a durability Class 2 in-ground species), with a service life of 15 years is what *Construction Timbers* calls a

---

[140] MacKenzie, Colin, C H Wang, R H Leicester, G C Foliente, M N Nguyen. *Timber service life design, Design guide for durability*. (Melbourne: Forest and Wood Products Australia Limited, 2020) 20.

"C4"[141] application and the minimum dimensions are to be 200x200 mm[142] and if a 50-year life is required it is a "C9"[143] application where a natural round of at least 400 mm diameter with sapwood treated to H5 is needed. If red ironbark is used (a durability Class 1 In-ground species) there is no minimum size for a 15-year design life but for longer, it requires a "C8"[144] application which is 300 mm natural round treated to H5.

For white cypress, the recommendations for 15 years are "C4" the same as spotted gum with 200x200 mm and "C15"[145] for a 50-year life which requires a 400 mm de-sapped piece despite both being durability Class 2 in-ground species. It differs to spotted gum as cypress cannot be treated successfully with waterborne preservatives. For Radiata there is no minimum size for either a 15 or a 50-year service life but the timber must be treated to H4 and H5 respectively. This reflects how well the preservatives work in sapwood but actually receiving sawn pine that meets this specification can be a challenge.[146]

The shortcoming of these recommendations is that a playground, if performing well and only needing minimal maintenance, should have a life well in excess of 15 years but changing trends will likely see it remodelled short of 50 years. So, Ted considers something in-between the two sizes may well be appropriate. Given that the posts are designed for a certain service life, it is probably prudent to clearly state on the drawings what that life is so it can be flagged that there must be a more thorough assessment than normal at that time.

Embedding Posts in the Ground
Common practice, at least with hardwood, is to set the posts in concrete but this is actually bad practice and is guaranteed to shorten the life of the timber. Ted was made aware of decay associated with mixing hardwood and concrete many years ago when he was supplying powerpoles.[147] Often this decay was aggravated by situations such as a domestic footpath where there was frequent watering and the addition of fertilizer. It is a situation many landscaping projects would experience though unlikely in a playground. As the timber shrinks, a gap develops between the post and the concrete so water and is trapped and fertilizer use in the vicinity promotes decay organisms. The problem is not solved by only specifying (and hopefully receiving) durability Class 1 in-ground timber. For all timber posts in-ground we recommend, at a minimum, backfilling with:

- Natural earth if suitable,
- Fine crushed rock; or,
- No fines concrete

---

[141] CTIQ, Vol 1 (Revised 2020), 26.
[142] Compare the table in CTIQ, Volume 2 where the Conditional use codes are given for each species for the design life required with Volume 1 where the minimum provision of that code is explained.
[143] CTIQ, Vol 1 (Revised 2020), 26.
[144] CTIQ, Vol 1 (Revised 2020), 26.
[145] CTIQ, Vol 1 (Revised 2020), 26.
[146] This should be read in conjunction with our comments on incising in the chapter, *Standards and Fitness for Purpose* and *Specifications* in the previous chapter
[147] One example Ted remembers is a 300 mm ironbark powerpole that was embedded in concrete rotting off after 14 years.

Ted's recommendation for no fines concrete follows that of Timber Queensland in its *Technical Data Sheet No. 9 Timber Retaining Walls for Residential Applications* where it says:

> "No fines concrete shall be 10mm maximum aggregate size, 450 kg cement per m^3 and a water cement ratio of 0.55. The concrete shall be ready mixed or hand mixed manufactured to the requirements of AS 1379. For no fines concrete the concrete shall be well agitated immediately before placing to ensure a complete coating of the aggregate. The concrete shall be discharged directly into the holes and tamped without delay. All concrete shall be placed within one hour of batching. The no fines concrete shall not be reworked as this destroys the bond."[148]

It further states (which is more important for free standing applications), "For no fines concrete, top the last 100mm with clay to prevent surface infiltration into the backfill." Note that to this specification, Ted would add, "Structural; posts should have a pole bandage added at ground level". Ralph would add that the post must be treated for rot and fungal attack and have a collar of painted "Diggers inground timber protection" or similar.

Pole Bandage and Rods

Even when using durability Class 1 in-ground timber, the life of posts can be extended by the use of a pole bandage as mentioned in the Timber Queensland guidelines. This product looks like a heavy-duty bubble wrap except that the bubbles are filled with preservative, mainly boron and fluorine. When there is moisture in the timber, the prerequisite for decay, the preservative is drawn into the timber. This product can add up to another five or even more years to the life of in-ground timber.[149] Note: A pole bandage should not be used to counter the effect of the bad practice of installing a post in concrete.

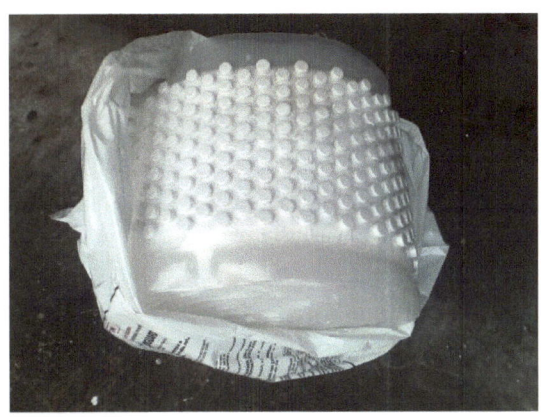

Figure 50.   Pole bandage.

Ted readily concedes that painted cypress posts with low sapwood content have been used successfully in fencing in the less challenging southern markets without a bandage, but a much higher design certainty is required for playground posts than for a fence post. It must also be conceded that cypress has been downgraded from in-ground 1 to in-ground 2 for a reason.

Shrink-wrap style bandages were developed by the CSIRO in the 1970's but Australian field trials proved that they created a microclimate under the bandage and hastened decay rather than delay it. These bandages are used and promoted in the UK where they are sold with a either a 20- or 40-year guarantee depending on the product.[150] Presumably, the climatic conditions make the difference.

---

[148] Timber Queensland. *Technical Data Sheet No. 9 Timber Retaining Walls for Residential Applications* (Brisbane: Timber Queensland. 2014) 5.

[149] One manufacturer of this type of product is Preschem (Australia) Pty. Ltd and is sold under the name *Bioguard Bandage*. This manufacturer claims its bandages are effective against white, brown and soft rot, an area where CCA has limited effectiveness.

[150] One such manufacturer is Postsaver Europe Ltd.

When an inspector is confronted with a playground that has already been constructed and has posts embedded in concrete, the opportunity of incorporating best practice has passed but they should be very aware of the risks involved. The posts should be diffused with polesaver rods or similar. When there is moisture in the timber the preservatives in the rods are drawn into the wood and so helps mitigate the effects of bad practice. This should be done at twice the recommended rate.[151] Subsequent inspections will involve checking the condition of the rod and probable replacement.

Method of Installation of the Post

The actual method of installing the post can vary. Figure 51 shows the normal recommendation but designers should refer also to Appendix A where more alternatives are provided by Ralph.[152] This arrangement has worked well but there are a few considerations. In Ted's home locality, the Lockyer Valley, ground line decay is predominantly in the top 450 mm and nothing much happens 600 mm deep and definitely nothing happened at 900 mm. But if you move further west where the topsoil is drier, it can be moister deeper down, the decay area likewise moves down and so the free draining gravel can then be important. A further consideration is that a gravel base does not suit a pre-cut post system. These must have a base of concrete or no fines concrete set to a predetermined level. Again, local knowledge is important as is a preparedness to be flexible depending on the product being used. An important consideration will be the ability to shed moisture sideways.

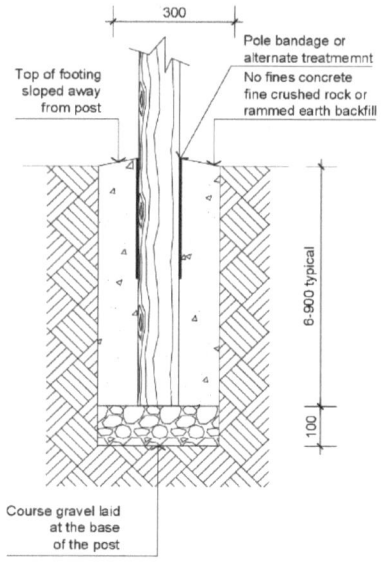

Figure 51. Normal recommendation for installing hardwood or cypress posts

What is seldom done but should be standard practice is the addition of extra decay protection at the groundline. This can be either with a pole bandage (refer Figure 50) or CN emulsion or other proprietary products. Refer to their guidelines for thickness of the coatings and the area to be treated.

Embedment Depth

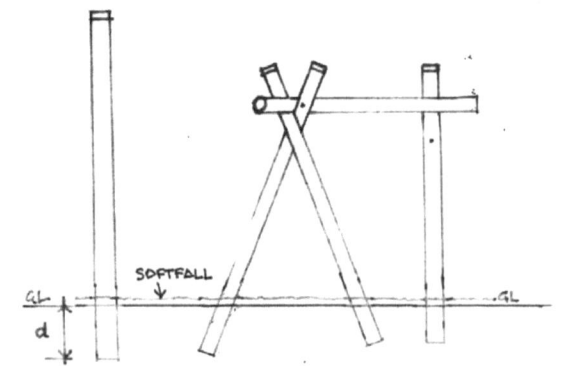

Figure 52. Don't underestimate the embedment depth requirements that may be attached to it

This chapter covers what Ted and Ralph consider to be best practice for engaging with the ground, but it intentionally does not discuss the embedment depth. The embedment depth ultimately is the responsibility of a structural engineer who should be detailing his design following our guidelines and final details will be dependent on:

- The soil conditions
- Whether it is free standing or self-supporting and braced
- The size and height of the post, and
- The load and movement imposed by any equipment

---

[151] Tingley, Dan. *Pers. Com.* April 22, 2021.
[152] Timber Queensland. *Technical Data Sheet 20, Residential Timber Fences.* (Brisbane: Timber Queensland. 2014) 2. Similarly, Bailey, Ralph. *Pers. Com.* 18 November 2015.

Notwithstanding, the depth will be significant, e.g., for an 8-metre overall length powerpole, the embedment in South East Queensland in good soil is 1.8 metres.[153] An inspector/certifier/engineer will need to question any freestanding post of any size or height that is only embedded 600 - 900 mm.

Posts in Supports

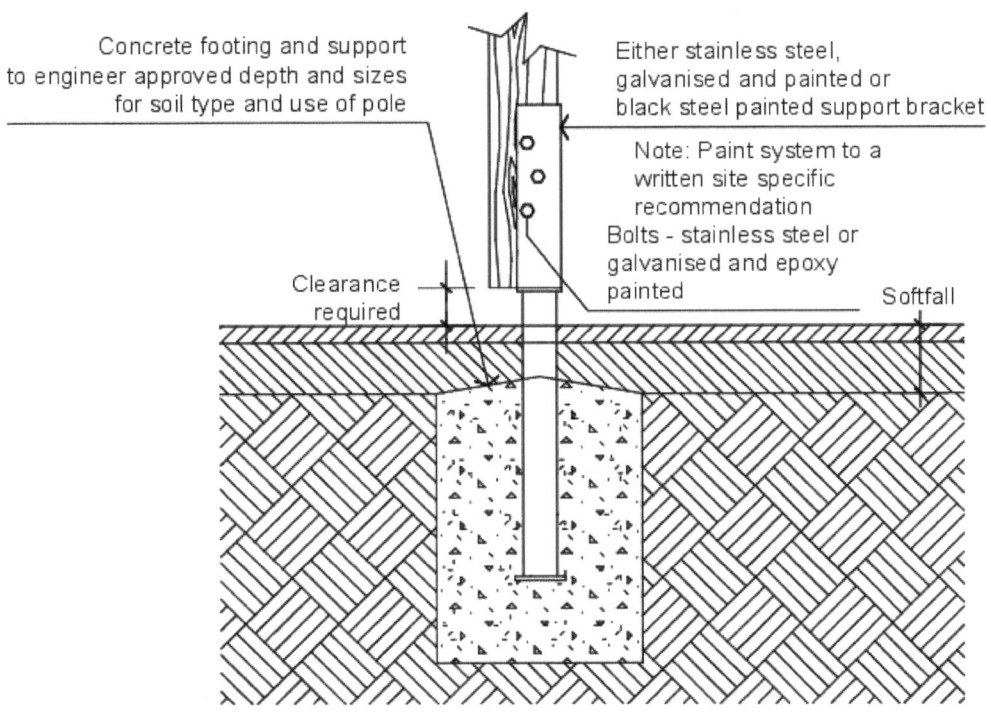

Figure 53.   Our guidelines for installing a post in a post support

---

[153] Energex. *Manual 00302 Overhead Design Manual*. (Brisbane: Energex. 2020) 10824-A4, Sect 2, Sub 3, sheet 1.

When timber is under the recommended size for embedment, it should be installed in stainless steel (ideally) post supports. However, there is little value going to a steel support if it is still inappropriate for the application. The danger is that a set of well-known problems can simply be swapped for ones that are different and less well understood. Figure 54 shows a durability Class 2 in-ground timber installed in a post support that is well below the surface. Decay can occur in the post above the bracket and the fasteners cannot be inspected. In our opinion the post supports with their associated fasteners should extend well above the undersurface as shown in Figure 53. In this way inground decay will not be an issue and the support and fasteners can be quickly inspected.

Figure 54. Post support terminates well under the top surface

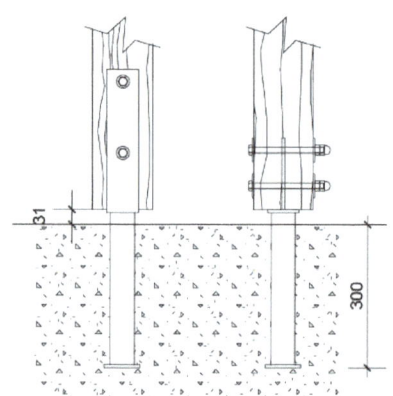

Figure 55. Standard supports normally only give one way resistance

Most "off the shelf" post supports (Figure 55) are made for verandah posts which are braced back to the main house through the roof structure. The connection at the ground does not need to be very heavy and, indeed, invariably they are not. At best, the commercially available brackets only offer stiffness in one direction. The supports in a playground need to offer resistance in all directions, and we have found that for sawn members, an exceptionally good way of doing this was with a custom fabricated metal support. Refer further option in Appendix A.

Illustrated in Figure 56 is the type of support used by Ted when operating Outdoor Structures Australia[154] and in this case for a 100 mm thick member. It is fabricated from a standard 100 mm C section. Note the use in this figure of screws and not bolts. There is nothing protruding on the other side and they always remain tight as there are no clearance holes and there is never any need to retighten. Predrilling is critical. Ralph's strong preference however is for bolts as there are less fasteners required and there is no overstressing of the screws should the builder fail to predrill.

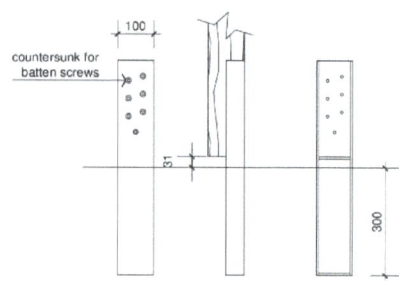

Figure 56. Post support fabricated from hot rolled C section as used by Ted

---

[154] This bracket is included as people familiar with Ted's work and his other publications would be aware of his use of this style of support. Ralph makes the case for an angle rather than a C section.

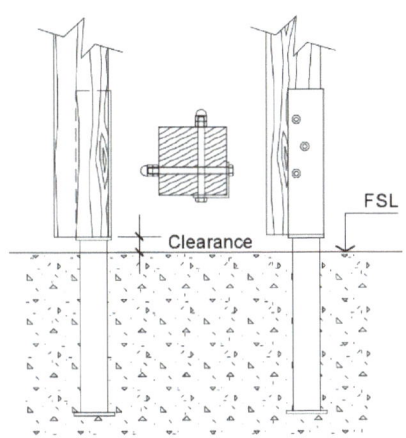

Figure 57. Alternate post support arrangement used by Ralph.

Instead of a C section, Ralph prefers an alternate means of achieving rigidity in all directions and this is done by using an angle iron support and in Figure 57 this is also added to a heavy pipe which also is equally as strong in all directions. This arrangement also avoids any problems with shrinkage as may be encountered with a hot rolled C section. The 31 mm measurement in both Figure 55 and Figure 57 is a suggested clearance above groundline during normal construction but in the case of a playground should be the minimum measurement above the softfall. Best practice would be to also seal the ends of the timber, and this can be done with CN emulsion or a wax-based sealant but being careful not to get excess on the sides of the timber. Paint will not adhere to these surfaces if these are present. Paint is discussed in the chapter *Inspection and Maintenance*.

Figure 58. Custom tool for fitting a pipe support to round timber

Figure 59. Example of a hole ready to take a pipe support

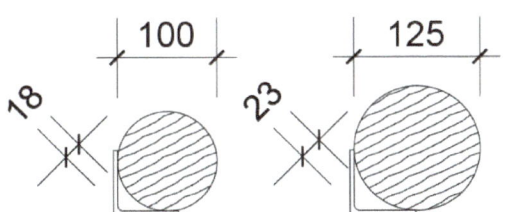

Figure 60. Finger entrapments in angle supports to parallel sided rounds

We do not recommend steel angles as a post support when used with round timber. While an angle iron support will work structurally on parallel sided logs, there is an issue with finger entrapment and also the corners should a child fall against them. Ted has drawn in Figure 60 a 65 mm equal angle fitted to a 100 mm and 125 mm true size log. The gap at the top is 18 and 23 mm respectively i.e., a finger entrapment. While this could easily be filled with a fillet of steel welded in place, natural round timber is not as easy to mount in a bracket. This is because it is not just "round", it is irregular and tapering. Commercial brackets again are generally not suitable. A system developed by the Forest Products Innovation of Agri-Science Queensland for joining powerpoles (Figure 58) could be modified to make a pipe base. The pipe could be secured either with appropriate fasteners or simply epoxied into place. This would require the ends to be sealed so moisture from the end grain did not affect the epoxy.

Blade type supports

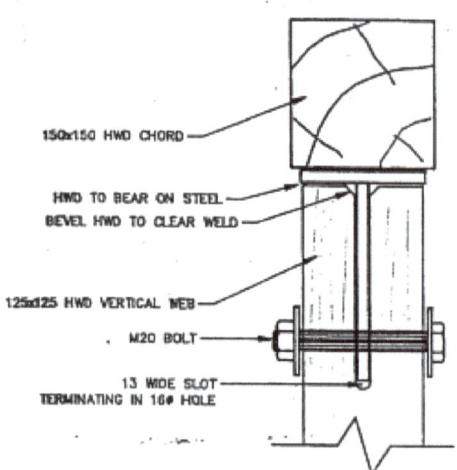

Figure 61. Well detailed blade type connection in a timber bridge made by Ted

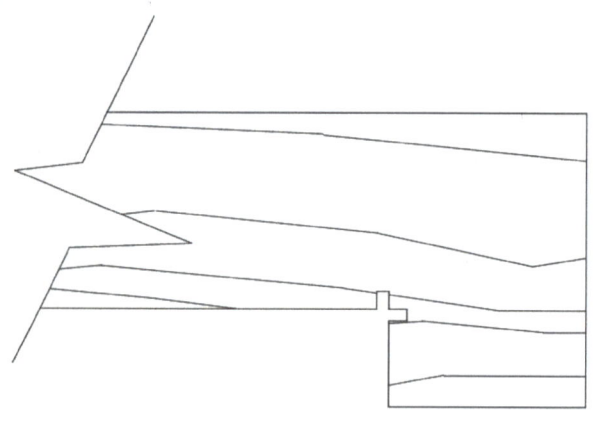

Figure 62. Poor building practice which involves cutting past the mark should not be accepted

Should a designer wish to use a blade type support on a playground post, it will generally need to be heavier than a domestic bracket and should be fabricated to a structural engineer's detail. The saw cut up the centre of the post to accommodate the support is likely to be in the order of 12 mm. There is the potential for the timber to continue to split from the end of that cut, especially if there is no clearance in the hole or the saw cut continues through.

A superbly detailed connection on a 125x125 hardwood web for one of Ted's bridges but in many regards similar to a blade type support is shown in Figure 61. Note the following:

- The blade is 12 mm but the cut is 13 mm
- The cut ends in a predrilled 16 mm hole which removed the stress point

The playground would differ in that, ideally, the timber would be in the order of 50 mm above the support plate for the blade. Note that cutting into a predrilled hole all but eliminates overcutting as illustrated in Figure 62.

Figure 63. Corrosion at groundline from water and concrete attacking galvanised steel.

Going from timber to steel at groundline simply swaps the potential for decay at groundline for corrosion at groundline. This corrosion can occur quickly. The hot dipped galvanized post in Figure 63 was only twelve years old when the image was taken and it is supporting a home, not a playground! While galvanizing can offer excellent corrosion resistance, surprisingly it can offer little resistance to pure rainwater.[155] Just as old, galvanized iron tanks had to have a protective film[156] so, similarly, galvanized posts must be protected at groundline and where it is in contact with concrete. In the past, this could have been done very effectively by tar epoxy paints. While it is best to paint the whole bracket, the minimum would be the full length below the groundline to just above it (say 50-100 mm), but it is easier to paint the whole item. These proven paints have now been removed from the market due to concerns they may have been a carcinogen. Replacement paints are produced which also give good protection.[157]

Corrosion can also occur between the steel and any timber member, and with hardwood in particular, due to its acidity. Ted's own practice would have been to apply a sacrificial epoxy paint coat[158] between the steel and the timber. This also applies to galvanised bolts in hardwood and pine, but our recommendation would be to paint these bolts and install in a slightly oversize hole but our preference is for stainless fasteners to avoid corrosion issues.

Figure 64.   Post support that appears to be made from 2 mm approx. Duragal[159] style material

Figure 65.   Corrosion, even though galvanised, in the same post support after 3 years

A further consideration is the thickness of the steel which, in turn, impacts the thickness of the galvanising. To reduce costs, the steel thickness can be reduced to as little as 3 mm or even less. We have even seen 2

---

[155] The *Lysaght Referee (27th edition)* makes an important observation when it says, "High purity rain-water. . . is aggressive to galvanised steel tanks" which must reasonably apply also to galvanised posts. (Sydney: John Lysaght. 1985).192.

[156] This was done by inserting a bag of chemicals called a *Tect-a tank* prior to any rainwater entering the tank.

[157] One such replacement paint used by Ted is PPG's *Sigmashield 880/Amerlock 880*, a two-component, high-build, polyamine adduct-cured epoxy coating while Ralph's preference is for Dulux *Durabuild STE epoxy* combined with *Dulux Weathermax HBR*. This is expanded on in the chapter on maintenance. These products are mentioned as a standard which should be met or exceeded by the paint you specify/use.

[158] The product we used was White Knight *Epoxy Enamel* in an aerosol as it was the only one available in our locality. It is important that it is not the normal decorative style paint.

[159] This opinion was determined by the surface finish and that the visible cut end had no galvanising on it.

mm! The effect is to reduce a total galvanizing thickness from 500 grammes per m² (GSM) for 4 mm thick steel to approximately 390 grammes for 3 mm. The impact of this is to reduce the published life expectancy from 33-100 years in a C3 medium risk[160] application to 26 to 78 years.[161] Both our practices would be not to use anything less than 4 mm. The published life expectancies are based on atmospheric corrosion rates and may not match real life expectancy as groundline corrosion is likely to be the governing influence. Ted could find no published guidelines for corrosion at groundline.

Should the application be in either of the higher risk C4 or C5[162] applications, galvanising would appear to be an imprudent choice based on the published life expectancy which is 17 to 33 years and 9 to 17 years respectively based on 4 mm steel. In these cases, stainless steel, (either 304 also known as A2 or 316 grade also known as A4) should be used.[163] Alternatively, appropriate timber installed correctly, and that is the challenge, will outlast galvanised steel unless it is of sufficient thickness and paint protected appropriately.

Figure 66.   Duragal style fence post

Duragal style products (only galvanised externally) or Supagal style (galvanised internally as well), in the opinion of Ted and Ralph, should not be used in any part of a playground as the coating thickness, which varies from 100 to 135 grammes per m²,[164] (and can be as low as 50)[165] is not sufficiently robust. This is much thinner than the already light coating you see on products such as Trip-L-Grips) which is generally rated to the Z275 category (275 GSM total for both sides). Products made to the Z275 specification are regularly recommended not to be used at all for exterior applications.[166] The guidelines for the use of "Tanalised" timber only allow timber to be used with Z275 galvanising if the position is at least 8 km from the coast (and presumably not embedded in concrete).[167]

As an example of what can go wrong, the steel post in Figure 66 is a *Duragal* type product installed directly in concrete without paint protection and is within metres of a swimming pool! As these can also be called a hot dipped galvanised product, it is important to specify the galvanised coating thickness on your product to avoid such light levels of galvanising. As mentioned, the epoxy paint coating is critical

---

[160] Described as "Atmospheric environment with medium pollution … e.g., urban areas, coastal areas with low deposition of chlorides". Galvanisers Association of Australia, *Atmospheric Corrosion Resistance of Hot Dipped Galvanized Coatings*. (Melbourne: Galvanisers Association of Australia. U.D) 6.

[161] Galvanisers Association of Australia. *Hot Dipped Galvanizing - The best protection inside and out*. (Melbourne: Galvanisers Association of Australia. U.D.) 6.

[162] Coastal areas without spray and coastal areas respectively. Galvanisers. *Atmospheric …*, 6.

[163] Pryda and other manufacturers require the stainless version of its steel products to be used within 10 km of the coast and Arch required stainless fitting to be used with timber treated with its waterborne chemicals when within eight km of the coast. See the full discussion in Ted's *Timber Preservation Guide*.

[164] OneSteel Trading. *DuraGal flooring* System – Issue 6. No publication details. 1.

[165] Orrcon Steel. *Datasheet – ALLGAL* Sept 2020 Rev 03 (no publication details) 1.

[166] Compare the 135 GSM to say a Z or C purlins, used under a roof which are normally to Z350 (175 GSM per side) or even Z450 (225 GSM per side) specification.

[167] This is discussed in detail under corrosion in Ted's *Timber Preservation guide*. Briefly, all timber is acidic to some degree, new preservatives are more corrosive, and some steel manufacturers will not warrant their steel used in conjunction with timber.

when steel is in contact with concrete externally. Simply upgrading from a light to heavy galvanised coating is still not a substitute for the additional protection of galvanised steel from corrosion by water and concrete.

Note: In Appendix 1, Ralph comments further on his observations relating to post supports.

Log seats and steppers

An inexpensive item to install in a timber playground can be simple offcuts of logs used as steppers or seats. They may not be inexpensive to maintain though, especially if they are set in concrete and installed in rubber softfall. In view of potential maintenance costs, a playground designer should consider whether these should be installed on a base also. Ralph's preference would be to do so and his method is shown in Figure 67

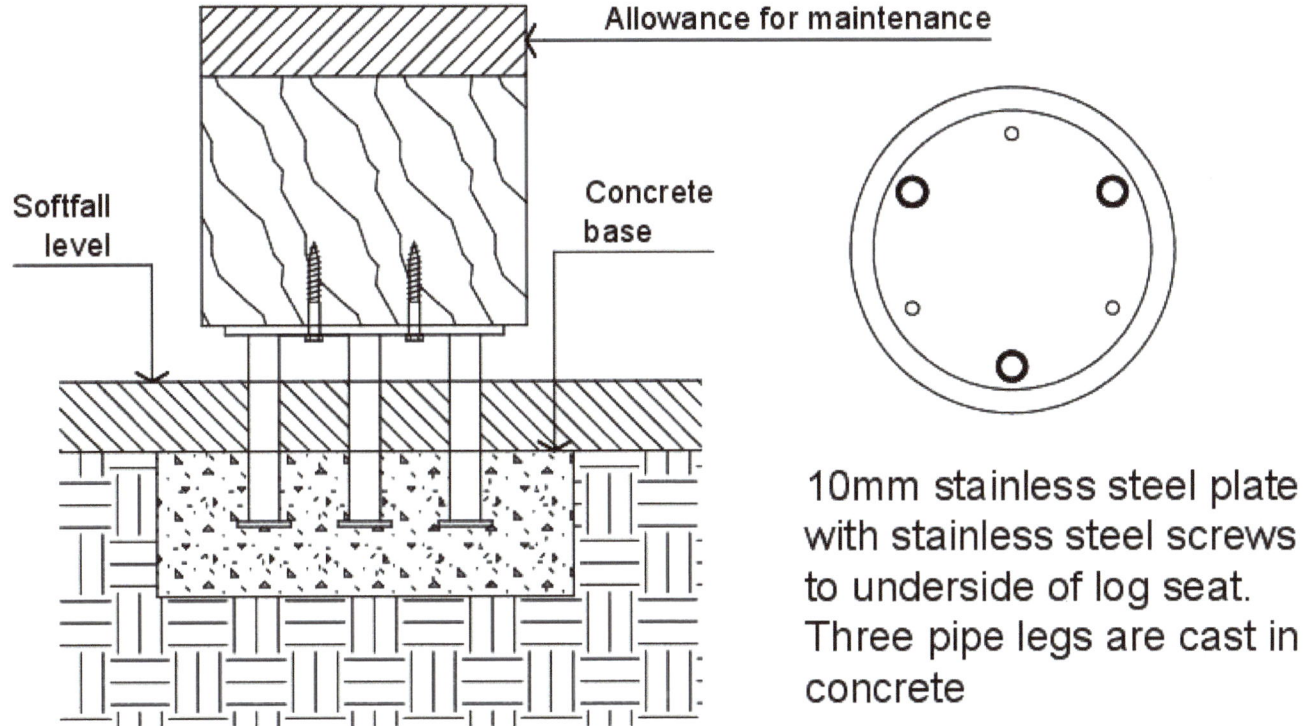

Figure 67.   Ralph's suggestion for installing log seats and stepping blocks

It is impossible to safely put a plate over the end to protect the end grain as any plate will be slippery when wet and likely to burn in summer. Degrade must be expected over time. Ted suggests that the overall length of any log seat also be installed say, 75mm longer than needed. This way it can be trimmed when the top is degrading.

Is galvanising even necessary?

We have recommended that galvanised steel has a protective paint coating but paint finishes have come a long way over recent decades. It is now possible to achieve an equivalent corrosion resistance to galvanised with an appropriate paint over black steel. Ralph would rather use the money that would have otherwise been spent on galvanising on heavier steel and bypass one process if the bracket is going to be painted anyway. As a former fabricator, Ted finds this attractive as the costs associated with galvanising are high. It is not just the costs per kilogram to galvanise but the lead time and freight both ways and even having to pay for long standing times just waiting to be loaded and unloaded at the galvanisers quickly mount up. Ted also has a number of items that have become dislodged during the coating process and are now sitting in the bottom of the galvanising bath, and that complicates matters having to remanufacture!

Further, both Ted and Ralph have had problems painting over galvanised steel. Generally, the steel is quenched in water after dipping but the oxides formed can cause difficulties with subsequent paint coats. The galvanisers must be advised not to quench, something easily forgotten at fabrication and galvanising. Some paint manufacturers will not warrant their paint on a galvanised surface. Ralph has had good experience with two pack polyurethane on black steel, bypassing the need for galvanising. Any paint specification you provide must be based on a written site-specific recommendation. Fabricators should avoid drilling through the support to form the bolt holes as this will damage the paint. They should only work on measurements on the timber.

Paint – general

Figure 68. "Blooming" on powder coated galvanised steel in C5 application.

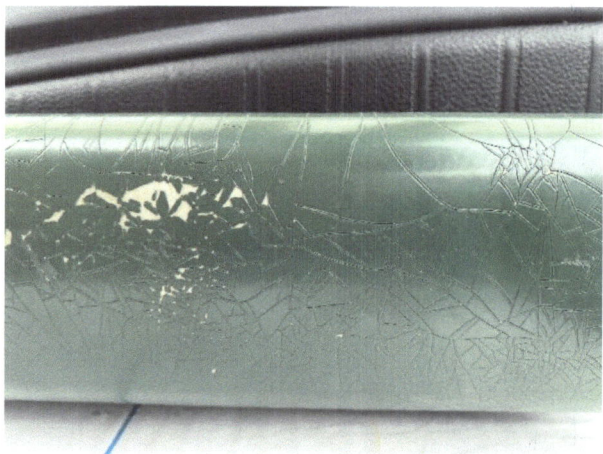

Figure 69. Powder coating flaking off steel.

Should a fully painted steel post support (or for that matter any item in the playground) be required, it can be done with brush, roller, spray or powder coating. What is applied is of more importance than how it is applied. Specifiers should avoid just saying "powder coated" or indeed any other generic painting term but seek a written site-specific recommendation for the preparation and a robust finish from the paint manufacturer.[168] Figure 68 illustrates this point and is from a bridge Ted supplied where the finish over the hot dipped galvanised rails was just mentioned as "powder coated" and it subsequently bloomed. The environment it was being used in required a very costly, high performing, specialty product and rectification was likewise expensive. You may consider including in your documentation that a certificate from the paint applicator be supplied stating that the coating meets the specification. Your considerations when deciding on a paint finish is that it can be touched up on site even if originally factory applied.[169].

Note: Paint is covered in more depth in the chapter *Inspection and Maintenance*.

---

[168] Ralph has had good results from Dulux *Armourspray*, a robust powder coating for long life on applications such as park seats, bins tree guards and railings etc. It is also anti-graffiti.
[169] A product preferred by Ralph for finishing steel or aluminium over a suitably primed substrate, that can be touched up on site, is *Dulux Weathermax HBR*.

Terminating timber paths

Figure 70. This termination is successful after 10 years despite being bad practice

Figure 71. Good practice for terminating a timber path as used by Ted

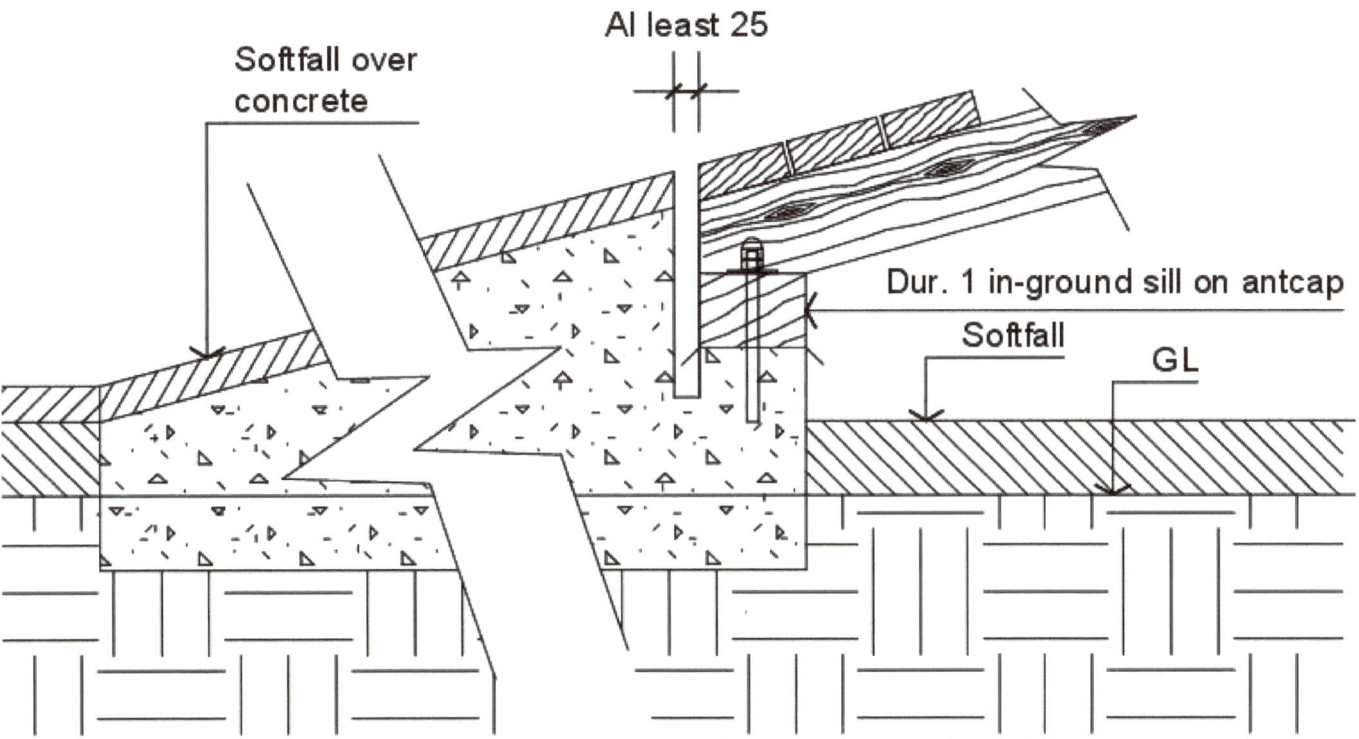

Figure 72. Alternate good prctice for ramp/softfall junction as used by Ralph

Some playgrounds will involve a section of timber path and generally it may be impractical to follow Ted's general guidelines for a boardwalk which requires at least 200 mm of ventilation under the timber (Figure 71). This boardwalk guideline is intended to deliver a structure with an intended service life far greater than a playground. The designer must adopt a "work around". The termination shown in Figure 70 is 10 years old and has no sign of decay or termites and that is because the timber is durability Class 1 in-ground and has natural termite resistant. Lesser timbers would not succeed in such a situation. Ralph's practice, as shown in Figure 72 is also to keep the timber out of ground contact. He terminates on a

Durability 1 in-ground sill which sits on an antcap. The groove behind the sill is intended to keep moisture away from the sill. The bearers at the end of the ramp closest to the ground should also be Durability 1 in-ground.

The designer should make every effort to detail the termination so it is above ground. Things to consider in the termination are:

- The concrete path will need to have at least R11 slip resistance (or even higher) and in some cases may need softfall rubber over it.
- Brackets should be stainless steel or galvanised and painted as described elsewhere in this guide
- The concrete should slope 25mm across the face to shed moisture
- The timber should be a minimum of 25, and ideally 50mm above the surface
- There should be a concrete back and side walls to stop soil encroaching.

In the end it simply may not be possible to design such an abutment. In this case, to some extent, even when the timber supply is appropriate an embedded termination may need to be considered sacrificial and accept it may eventually need replacement.

7 FASTENERS

General Considerations

A playground may be built with appropriate timber but be let down through the wrong choice of fasteners or incorrect installation processes. It is unlikely that the fastener will fail due to being inappropriately sized as generally, the loadings are quite light considering the capacity of even a new 10 mm bolt. Incorrect fastener choice (combined with poor maintenance) can impact a playground through either corrosion requiring a rebuild of the structure or personal injury to a child as a result of something as simple as a bolt losing its nut through vandalism or working loose. It will be recommended that all fasteners in playgrounds should be a minimum of 304 grade stainless from a major manufacturer[170] or otherwise 316 grade.

Figure 73.   Diecast "Touchnuts"

Figure 74.   Dangerous Protruding bolts

When Ted first started making barbecue tables in 1985, he heard a story about how a child climbed under a table and while playing there, cut her face badly on a protruding bolt. The payout was substantial as it should have been. He resolved that his items would be free of protruding bolts (Figure 74) so mainly he used coachscrews to assemble the frame. He first started building bridges in the same year and there was then little specialised hardware that was readily available, so he used a barrel nut called a *Touchnut*[171] shown in Figure 73. He purchased this product from a playground manufacturer. After a time, this diecast nut was taken off the market and replaced with a stainless-steel version with a mushroom head. Ted was told a story of how a child was injured when the nut stripped out and the piece of timber it was securing came adrift. What was seen as a good idea at the time was anything but. Ted also observed how these nuts would corrode badly when his barbecue tables were situated near the coast. They were not fit for purpose.

Ralph became aware of corrosion of galvanised bolts in CCA treated pine play structures some years ago when he constructed a CCA pine log playframe including swing set, lookout, climbing net, tyre swing and slide for his own children. After a couple of years, he chose to dismantle the play area and relocate it. He was astounded that the large M10 hot dipped galvanised bolts (installed horizontally) and pigtail bolts

---

[170] Ted was aware of fasteners sold as but not complying with 304 grade being sold in Australia. The argument for 304 as the minimum is made in his book Timber Joints and is not repeated here. Ted's decision is based on long term testing by BRANZ in costal applications in New Zealand.

[171] The term can still be used to describe a stainless-steel version presently on sale. The two products are not to be confused.

(installed vertically through the beam) had almost corroded right through and large pine logs could have fallen and/or pigtail bolts failed. Ralph believed then (and discussed with Ted at the time) that extreme care is needed if galvanised bolts are to be used, instead of stainless-steel, in timber exposed to the weather. The minimum he would accept then for bolts through CCA or hardwood would be to slightly oversize the hole, dip the bolts in two pack epoxy and touch up the nut and thread afterwards. Fortunately, since then stainless has become much more readily available. Another example he saw that affirmed his opinion was a simple picnic shelter at a coastal beach and all of the galvanised gangnail plates had corroded and become loose and shaky and barely holding the shelter together. Everything exposed to the weather should have been stainless.

Likewise, for a playground designer, of utmost importance when considering fasteners is the safety of the users and fitness for purpose. The type, size and material of fasteners available now is much greater today be warned, the quality of many fasteners is considered to have been greater when fasteners were made in this country. In 2012 Ted met with an experienced playground designer at the end of her professional life. She told him how she had been using 12 mm pigtail bolts[172] to attach swings for all her career. They were made in Australia and were trouble free, then a contractor used a lower cost imported product. After some time, despite being 12 mm, it broke, and the child was injured, and she was facing the legal consequences. Without proof testing as you would say of a lifting chain, how can designers know if they are purchasing a product that not only looks right but is right.

Outside of tested product, which would be prohibitively expensive, there is no easy answer to this problem, but the following guidelines for the use and specification of fasteners will help:

- Use specialised vandal resistant hardware that cannot be substituted with domestic products purchased from the local big box hardware store.
- Ensure that the structural integrity cannot be compromised by the failure of a single bolt or screw.
- Only specify items from specialised suppliers that have independent quality checks, and not just at the factory, which will most likely be in China.[173]

Fastener Material Type
Correctly galvanised fasteners, such as nailplates, in sealed roof spaces have proven satisfactory as the moisture content of the timber quickly drops to below 20% so decay is not an issue and as there is no ongoing wetting and drying of the timber, corrosion is not usually an issue. They are even now permitted in roof cavities right by the beach[174] though Ralph would question the wisdom of this. This, however, is far removed from a playground application. Even when a shade sail is installed the fasteners are not protected and moisture will be an issue. When Ted was researching his book, *Timber Joints* he found a wide variety of recommendations about the material that was recommended for fasteners in weather

---

[172] These are no longer used but the issue of a low-cost (quality?) fastener not being able to carry even a light load is the issue.
[173] The quality of some "over the counter" Chinese fasteners is discussed in Ted's guide, *Timber Joints*.
[174] Pryda Australia. *Technical Update, Corrosion Resistance of Pryda Products*. (Dandenong South: Pryda Australia. 2015) 3.

exposed applications in treated timber. That book has a detailed chapter explaining why, for Ted and Ralph, stainless is the material of choice for any fasteners in a timber structure exposed to the weather. The reader should refer to that book if further information is required. Factors that can impact on corrosion in a playground are:

- pH of the species of timber selected
- The moisture content of the timber
- Preservative treatment
- Environmental considerations
- The presence of decay, and
- Fastener material and quality

Species	pH	Trouble
Blackbutt	3.6	yes
Mountain ash	4.7	no
Ironbark, red narrow leaf	4.0	yes
Spotted gum	4.5	no
Rose gum	5.1	no
Jarrah	3.3	yes
Radiata	4.8	no
Cypress	5.4	no

Table 15.   Corrosion from acidity of timber.[175]

If the joint is to be exposed to any moisture, the acidity of the timber must be considered. Corrosion can be an issue when the Ph drops below 4.3. While the pH of a piece of timber varies within the piece and from piece to piece there are published values which can be used as a guide (refer Table 15). If the specification is just, say, "F14" it has to be assumed that a species with a lower pH will be supplied. By nominating a species outside of the problem range, such as spotted gum, the consequences of corrosion can be minimised.

Given the relatively benign chemistry of wood it can appear a simple environment where corrosion is not a challenge but wood "has a complex interaction with water that greatly affects its physical and chemical properties including corrosion."[176] Wood is a hydrophilic material meaning it has a strong affinity with water and some species can absorb up to 200% of their dry mass as water. This water can be either free liquid water or water vapour in the cells and cavities or bound water held by intermolecular forces in the cell walls. The point where the free water is expelled, and only bound water is present is called the fibre saturation point and is normally about 30% moisture content. In service, moisture is given off and taken in freely until it reaches equilibrium with its environment.[177] Below a moisture content of 15-18% embedded fasteners do not corrode but will start to increase around 20% and reach a maximum corrosion rate at or above fibre saturation point.[178] This is the situation that playground fasteners must deal with.

Another factor that impacts upon corrosion when fasteners are weather exposed is the preservative used. Newer preservatives ACQ and Tanalith E (also called copper azole or CuAz) have proven effective replacements for CCA as far as timber decay is concerned. But without the chrome and arsenic, these alternative chemicals require a significantly higher level of copper in the timber than with CCA. A higher

---

[175] This table is drawn from Bootle, Keith R. *Wood in Australia, Types, properties and uses, Second Edition*. (North Ryde: McGraw Hill Australia, 2005), 60-1 and Table 2.3.3 of Forests and Wood Products Australia. *Manual 6 – Embedded corrosion of fasteners in exposed timber structures*. (Melbourne. Forest and Wood Products Australia: 2007). On this scale a pH of 0 is highly acidic, 7 is neutral and 14 is highly alkaline. The scale is logarithmic with a 10-fold jump between each unit.
[176] Zelinka. *Corrosion ...*, 568.
[177] Zelinka. *Corrosion ...*, 568.
[178] Zelinka. *Corrosion ...*, 574.

concentration of water soluble copper is "more likely to initiate serious corrosion of susceptible metallic components embedded in or in contact with these timbers".[179] Corrosion could be from four to nine times that of CCA over a one year period.[180] The iron and hydroxyl ions released from the corrosion attacks the cellulose components of the timber causing "nail sickness" whereby there is significant loss in the structural integrity of the joint.[181] By contrast, it has been argued that the chrome and/or arsenic of CCA can have a passivating effect on fasteners.[182]

Fig. 19. Sons of Gwalia head rig.

A further factor that will influence the choice of fasteners is the climate. The Australian climate is very varied, from hot humid tropics to dry deserts. The heritage listed head rig from the Sons of Gwalia mine at Gwalia (a two-hour drive north of Kalgoorlie) in Western Australia in the Great Victoria Desert was built during 1886-8 from 300x300 Oregon pine. About a third has been replaced with kauri which is not a great deal more durable (in-ground durability Class 3) but basically the timber has lasted ten times longer than you would normally expect. The bolts are just black steel without any corrosion protection and they, just like the timber, have survived because there is seldom any moisture. Invariably, playground designers will have to deal with the effects of a more, and even much more aggressive and unforgiving environment.

Considering all these factors, our recommendation would have to be for stainless steel[183] unless you can be certain that the playground will be replaced in say a maximum of ten years. Your drawings would need to state this. As for the grade of stainless, the long-term exposure field trials conducted by BRANZ in New Zealand has demonstrated that 304 grade is suitable for a design life in excess of 15 years and up to 50 years.[184] If you can be certain of receiving 304 grade it is acceptable but will be subject to tea staining which can, in some instances, be desirable as it makes the fasteners less pronounced. Otherwise use 316 grade.

Vandal Resistance
While appropriate vandal resistant fasteners may initially add significant cost, their value to the asset owner through reduced harm to the public cannot be quantified. As well, vandal resistant fasteners would

---

[179] Li, Z.W., N.J. Marston and M.S. Jones. *Corrosion of Fasteners in Treated Timber Study Report SR241 2011* (Branz, 2011), i
[180] Li. *Corrosion ...*, i. Initially corrosion was thought to more than double that of CCA. Bootle. *Wood ...*, 62. Simpson Strong-Tie after testing 2600 samples assessed them as a little more than double. Anon, *Preservative Treated Wood Technical Bulletin No. T-PRWOOD08-R* (Pleasanton: Simpson Strong-Tie. 2008), 3. This assessment was based on accelerated weathering tests based on the American Wood-Preservers Association's *Standard E12-94 Standard Method for Determining Corrosion of Metal in Contact with Treated Wood*.
[181] Li. *Corrosion ...*, ii.
[182] Rammer, Douglas, Samuel Zelinka, Philip Line. *Fastener Corrosion: Testing, Research and Design Considerations*, a paper given at World Conference on Timber Engineering 2006, 1.
[183] This agrees with the detailed requirements for threated timber provided by Arch Wood Protection, Inc. *Hardware Recommendations for treated Wood*. (Arch Wood Protection, Inc. and Arch Treatment Technologies, Inc. 2006.)
[184] Li. *Corrosion ...*, 66.

be expected to deliver significant benefit over the structure's life even if the reduced maintenance and park closures was the only consideration. One manufacturer of security fasteners noted that property damage itself fosters an environment that encourages "further crime and decay. Safe, functional spaces help maintain civil order."[185]

Vandal resistance will also be mentioned in discussion of the broad categories of fasteners but not all fasteners offer the same protection. One manufacturer recognises three levels of protection:

- **Level 1.** Protection is offered against opportunistic vandalism, but fasteners can still be removed with commonly available tools
- **Level 2.** Fasteners can only be removed using special tools, the distribution of which can be controlled, and
- **Level 3.** Once fasteners have been installed there is no tool for removing them.[186]

The normal stainless batten screw with a hexagon drive as shown in Figure 80 would be classed as a Level 1 fastener but after they have been installed in hardwood at least, they are very hard to remove. These screws would not usually be subject to opportunistic vandalism but a bolt with a countersunk head is extremely easy to remove with a simple socket set. Probably the most common fastener used on playgrounds is an internal Torx drive incorporating an internal pin (Figure 75). Strictly this only offers Level 1 resistance but is popular because of its lower cost. At the other end of the scale, some Level 3 fasteners may be unsuitable for playgrounds as they may either be too light[187] or may leave a protruding thread as with the conical nut. The use of these nuts would be restricted to applications such as a "double nut" used on an attachment point well above the reach of children. So, apart from batten screws in hardwood, the playground designer, while mindful of the additional cost, would be advised to concentrate on fasteners that provide Level 2 protection.

Figure 75.   Level 1 vandal resistant fasteners using internal Torx drive with a centre pin

---

[185] Sentinel Group. n.d. *Fastener Safety Levels and Why They're Vital to Public Safety*. Accessed February 10, 2021. https://blog.sentinelgrp.com.au/fastener-security-levels-and-why-theyre-vital-to-public-safety/.
[186] Sentinel. *Fastener …*,
[187] Ted used 8# screws with one-way heads to attach the stainless caps to his bollards but in reality, they could be easily sheared off using a screwdriver and hammer.

Figure 76. Level 2 vandal resistant fasteners require restricted tools

Figure 77. Level 3 vandal resistant fasteners cannot be undone once tightened (blade screwdriver only drives one way)

Figure 78. Level 3 vandal resistant fasteners cannot be undone once tightened (hex nut breaks off after tightening)

Some Observations Regarding Fasteners

Coachscrews

Ted has concerns about using coachscrews, or at least 10 mm coachscrews and definitely for even smaller sizes, given the number that he has snapped off making barbecue tables. Figure 79 shows the actual dimensions of a 10x75 mm coachscrew. Over only 4 mm, the shaft goes from 8 to 10 mm. The screws always broke where the thread ended. His concern is that there is a possibility of the fastener being stressed during assembly and fail in service. They are also more prone to vandalism as a simple socket set is all that is needed to remove them. Note that the timber must always be countersunk for the head and the washer.

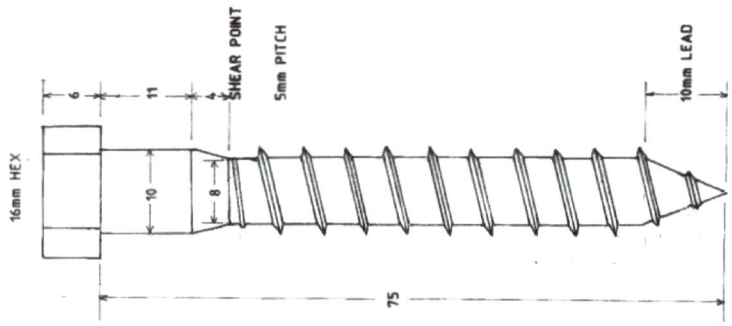

Figure 79. Dimensions of a 75x10 mm coachscrew

More is said about a substitute screw in the section on custom fasteners.

Self-drilling Type 17 screws

The introduction of Type 17 self-drilling screws revolutionised screw use in Australia. A powerful drill could simply force a 14# x 75 mm screw into hardwood without predrilling. This is how contractors have learnt to use this type of screw and it can do a lot of damage to the timber. A concern Ralph has with screws is that because they can be forced in with no predrilling, they can be stressed with the potential for failure.

Better construction practices are needed for playgrounds. Instead of using brute force, a hole must be fully predrilled and a lubricant such as CN emulsion or a wax should be applied. Screws must be in a staggered alignment to avoid splitting (Figure 80) and edge clearances of at least 4 diameters need to be maintained.

Figure 80.   Screws have split the joist

It should be noted that in 2105, *AS 3566 – Self Drilling Screws* was withdrawn. This Standard was unusual as it is a performance-based specification and not a materials specification. While major manufacturers are still supplying to this standard there is no guarantee that all manufacturers are, and we can probably be certain that some aren't.

Barrel Nuts

Barrel nuts, available as either countersunk or mushroom head are an excellent way of avoiding the dangers of a protruding thread on timber play structures. The ones Ted used were M12 and that size is not as readily available as M10. The length of the tube is generally sufficient to allow for free thread that can be used to take up any shrinkage that may occur. A minimum of 10 -12 mm of free thread is required at time of construction. Note that the nuts in Figure 81 have a simple hex drive but were available with a pin in the centre and needed a special Allen key socket. We found however that the pin was very easily broken off and its deterrent value was only in perception rather than reality. An internal Torx drive, with or without the pin, would offer improved vandal resistance. Most vandalism is spur of the moment and the less common the tool required, the less likely is the chance of vandalism.

Figure 81.   M12 stainless barrel nuts

Figure 82. Missing (and replaced) barrel nuts

Figure 83. Barrel nuts from underneath

Two-barrel nuts can often be found used in conjunction with a section of threaded rod as in Figure 82 and Figure 83. Ted found that with time, after seasoning of the timber, barrel nuts started to sit proud of the timber and were prone to occasional vandalism as is clearly seen in Figure 82. It is important in a playground setting that a *Locktite* style thread locker be used in conjunction with the nut.

Brad hole T nut

A nut that has been used successfully in shelter sheds is a "brad hole T nut." This nut should not be used in a playground where there is unseasoned timber. It differs from a tube nut in that there is a shorter length of thread, (it may be no more than an ordinary nut) and the end is open. Assuming you are joining a 125 mm thick spotted gum post to a 50 mm member, and with 6% shrinkage there will be 10 mm shrinkage to accommodate.

In this situation, the thread is either likely to be barely engaged with the nut when assembled or, after fastening, the thread will protrude. Both possibilities can cause injury.

Figure 84. Brad hole T nut used on seasoned pine

Nail Plates

Figure 85.   External nail plate being forced out

Nail plates allow for the quick prefabrication of sawn timber components. While stainless plates may be suitable for use in a shade structure which has sufficient height where there is no possibility of a child being in contact with them, there is no situation where they can be used in the play equipment itself. Constant wetting and drying forces the plates out of the timber exposing sharp edges. When they are sitting 2-3 mm proud of the surface the holding ability is halved.

Custom fasteners.

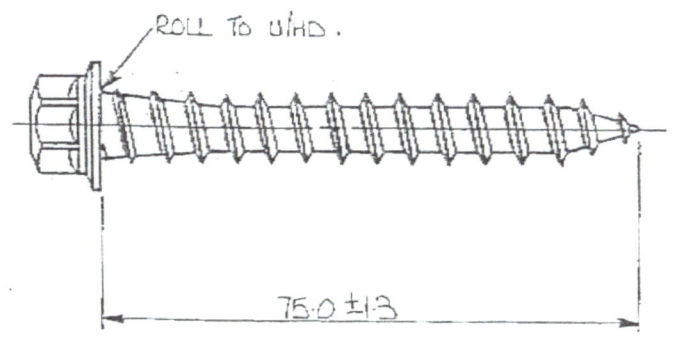

Figure 86.   Ted's patented Landscape Screw.

Having fasteners made to order to meet a specific need can be a reasonable approach. When Ted experienced troubles with the standard coachscrew he had his own screws manufactured. He called it the Landscape Screw. It was heavily galvanised, in high tensile steel with an external Torx head and very importantly, a patented thread.[188] It solved all his problems till the manufacturer ceased trading.

Production of custom fasteners is much easier now than when the Landscape Screw was developed meaning designers are even less restricted to off the shelf fasteners. If your desired specialty fastener is not available from a manufacturer, now with CNC lathes being readily available, it is possible and even relatively economical to design your own. The grade frequently chosen in stainless is SAF2205[189] which has high mechanical strength, roughly twice that of authentic stainless steel. You will just have to purchase a full bar which is available in lengths from 4 to 6 metres long and in diameters up to 150 mm. Forming Allan key heads is not difficult, while others may be available on request.

---

[188] The patent has now expired. Drawings are available by contacting Ted.
[189] This is a Sandvik code but is well recognized in the industry. Sandvik say of this duplex stainless steel that it is "characterized by high resistance to stress corrosion cracking (SCC), pitting, crevice and general corrosion and very high mechanical strength." URL: http://www.smt.sandvik.com/en-au/products/trademarks/sandvik-saf-2205/ Date accessed. June 24, 2015.

8 CONSTRUCTION DETAILS

As this guide has progressed through the different chapters, a number of construction details have been discussed as they arose as a consequence of the discussion e.g., *Engaging with the Ground* and *Fasteners*. This chapter is therefore brief and only touches on matters not directly mentioned already.

Decking

Fastening from underneath

Face fixing of decking is so embedded in timber decking construction that it is easily overlooked that it is not best practice as it often results in the joists splitting and moisture entering the joist with resulting decay. Whenever possible, decking should be fastened from underneath.

Thicker decking suits prefabrication incorporating stainless steel angles. Laser cutting which allows for slotted holes and computerised folding make the fabrication of these very simple. The angles that Ted used were 50x50x5 mm, 304 stainless in conjunction with 14# screws. Fastening 19 mm decking from underneath is not as straightforward as there simply is not sufficient length of screw holding the decking. A proprietary product, *Deckmaster* by Grabber Construction Products is a secret nail system which installs the screws at an angle so giving the necessary length of embedment. This product or similar is an option.

Face Fixing.

Your decking thickness dictates the screw size and that in turn dictates the joist width. A 35 mm deck requires a 14# (6.15 mm) hexagonal drive[190] countersunk stainless screw with a minimum grade of 304 stainless and that requires a 75 mm joist so screws can be installed on say a 16 mm minimum stagger and still maintain the required edge clearance. A 35 mm thick deck needs a 75 mm screw and 45 mm decking needs 85 mm minimum, but it is likely only 100 mm is available. The screws need to be fully predrilled. Unseasoned decking is laid tight with a target gap dictated by the decking width and the percentage shrinkage of the species used and seasoned is laid with a gap of say 3 mm. Ensure the width to thickness of the decking does not exceed 3.5:1.

Decking that is 19-21 mm thick must be seasoned meaning it is always laid with a gap. Do not exceed 90 mm wide to avoid cupping. This decking can be secured with a 10# screw and sufficient stagger can be achieved on a 50 mm joist. Predrilling is generally optional, except at the ends, but will be necessary with the hardest hardwoods.

---

[190] Ted found that internal torx drive were very hard on drive bits when being used on Australian hardwood.

 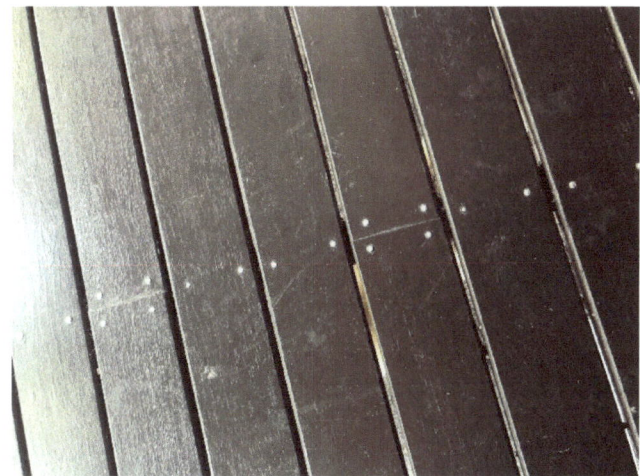

Figure 87.   Nail withdrawing from decking exposed to the weather

Figure 88.   Dome headed nails cannot be sanded over

We do not recommend fastening decking in playgrounds with nails. Apart from the fact that builders do not stagger their alignment., when they are in full sun they are forced out of the timber by the constant moisture changes in the timber. The nail in Figure 87 is on the outermost board in the verandah on Ted's home. Dome headed nails which are frequently used cannot be sanded over should the decking need to be refreshed.

A dampcourse such as *Gtape* should be used. Normally Ted and Ralph would recommend an aluminium strip with a tar back such as *Byuteflash* or *Flashtac,* but this may have a sharp edge which must be avoided in this setting. Ted no longer recommends Malthoid. As mentioned in the specifications chapter, the decking should have a rough sawn and coarse sanded face for grip, pencil rounded edges to avoid splinters and be processed so the best face is upwards. The width to thickness ratio of the decking is ideally a maximum of 4 to 1 for seasoned (though 88x19 and 88x21 have proved successful) and 3.5 to 1 for unseasoned.

Note: fastening to steel needs more thought as there can be issues with protruding screws and many screw manufacturers do not certify their screws going from timber to steel, at least when face fixed. At the time of writing there are no 14# screws in stainless available as they are too soft to drill and thread steel. There are options for 10# where bi-metallic screws can be sourced. These have a hardened steel tip welded to the stainless. The designer should obtain a written recommendation from the manufacturer. Alternately, safety and vandal resistant fittings should be used. Remember the sacrificial paint coat on the steel under the decking.

Changes of direction

Figure 89. Mitres can introduce sharp points and should be avoided

Figure 90. Tapered decking gives safer changes of direction

When there are changes of direction in the deck, often the easiest way to do it is with mitred decking. This should be avoided however, as the sharp end, which is often unrestrained over a considerable distance can raise and become a spearing object for a bare foot (Figure 89). Tapered decking (with a minimum end size of 70 mm will avoid this possibility (Figure 90). To ensure that this happens as intended, detailed drawings may need to be produced of both the joist layout and the arrangement of the tapers.

Note: When detailing a deck similar to that shown in Figure 90, the joists should have a minimum of 25 mm overhang and a maximum of 150 mm.

Edge Treatment
Splinters in rough sawn timber are invariable found on the corners while the edge of square dressed timber are very sharp and can cause injury. Frequently playground timber is arrised using a power plane, but this is not recommended as instead of one edge that can splinter the asset owner ends up with two. Edges and ends should be pencil rounded using a router to remove the corner.

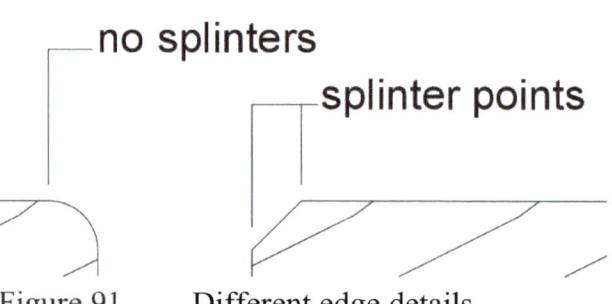
Figure 91. Different edge details

Ted's practice was to use a 6 mm rounding over bit on sizes up to 150 mm and 10mm on larger sizes.

Mitre joints

Ted has observed that mitre joints should be avoided. The issue has been that material can collect in the joint and cause them to open up. The example in Figure 92 has a gap that could potentially trap fingers. Better practice would be to pass one length through to the end and then butt the adjoining piece into it but leaving a 3-4 mm gap so moisture cannot enter the end grain.

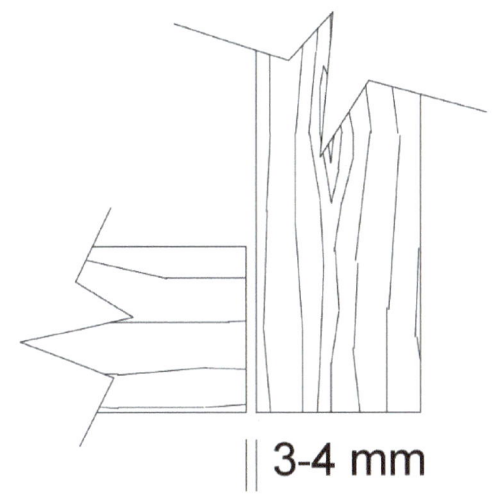

Figure 92. Mitre joint being forced open

Figure 93. Butt joint detail

End sealing
All end grain should be sealed. Ted would use CN emulsion in his bridges and boardwalks but then is little possibly of contact with children. The MSDS expressly forbids contact with children so, other for sealing the end of a natural round which is then capped and the bottom of posts, it should not be used. With CN emulsion out of the question outside of capping it is difficult to recommend an effective a long-term end sealant.[191] A paraffin wax emulsion as used as a log end sealer is probably the only solution.

End and Edge Clearances
It is critical that the correct end clearances are maintained. In tension, the bolt should be 8 diameters from the end though Ted's practice was to add an extra 50 mm to allow for weathering when used externally. Sometimes, it takes a lot of thought to be able to achieve the necessary end clearance. Spacings for screws is much simpler than bolts as it does not matter what the timber thickness is or whether it is seasoned or not, the distance remains the same (Table 16).

---

[191] Ted discussed this with Jack Norton, Secretary of the Timber Preservers Association of Australia and to his knowledge also there is no effective sealant outside of CN Emulsion. His practice would be to physically cap it after applying emulsion.

Spacing Location	Code Requirement D = Screw Diameter	E.g., 6.3 mm dia. Screw (14 gauge)
End Distance	10D	10 x 6.3 = 63 mm
Edge Distance	5D	5 x 6.3 = 32 mm
Between screws along grain	10D	10 x 6.3 = 63 mm
Between screws across grain	3D	3 x 6.3 = 19 mm

Table 16. Minimum screw spacings.[192]

The requirements for bolts are given in Table 17.

Load	Unseasoned	Example 12mm bolt	Seasoned	Example 12mm bolt
Loads parallel to grain				
Edge distance	2D	2 x 12 = 24 mm	2D	2 x 12 = 24 mm
End Distance in tension	8D	8 x 12 = 96 mm	7D	7 x 12 = 84 mm
End Distance in compression	5D	5 x 12 = 60 mm	5D	5 x 12 = 60 mm
End Distance with bending movement	5D	5 x 12 = 60 mm	5D	5 x 12 = 60 mm
Distance between bolts along grain	5D	5 x 12 = 60 mm	5D	5 x 12 = 60 mm
Distance between bolts across grain	4D	4 x 12 = 48 mm	4D	4 x 12 = 48 mm
Loads perpendicular to grain – worked example for 12mm bolt[193]				
Edge distance			4D	4 x 12 = 48 mm
End distance			5D	5 x 12 = 60 mm
Distance between bolts along grain	25 mm thick	b/D ratio 2.08	2.6 D	2.6 x 12 = 31mm
	38 mm thick	b/D ratio 3.95	3.22D	3.2 x 12 = 38 mm
	50 mm thick	b/D ratio 4.16	3.85D	4 x 12 = 48 mm
	75 mm thick	b/D ratio 6.25	5D	5 x 12 = 60 mm
	100 mm thick	b/D ratio 8.33	5D	5 x 12 = 60 mm
Distance between bolts across grain			5D	5 x 12 = 60 mm
Loads acting at an angle of 0-30° to the grain			As for loads parallel to grain	
Loads acting at an angle of 30° to 90° to the grain			As for loads perpendicular to grain	

Table 17. Bolt spacings.[194]

---

[192] Standards Australia. *AS 1720.1 – 2010* …, Section 4.5.4 and Table 4.4.

[193] For other sizes divide b with is the thickness of the member by D which is the bolt diameter (b/D). For a ratio of 2, the distance between the bolts along the grain is 2.5 times the diameter. The distance is pro rata until a ratio of 6 or more is achieved and then the distance is 5D. That is an increase in .625D for each ratio increase. For an M20 bolt fixing a 100 mm thick member the b/D ratio is 5. The distance is the base of 2.5D plus 3 times .635D = 4.37D which equals 87.5 mm say 90 mm.

[194] Derived from Standards Australia *AS 1720.1 – 2010*, Sections 4.4.4.2 ,4.4.4.3 and 4.4.4.4.

Connecting Timber

When connecting two pieces of timber, common practice is to check, say, the post and house the bearer into it. The thought is that the ledge can carry any load imposed on the bearer but come back after six months and it is simply hanging off the bolt with a gap underneath. In service, invariably the timber is carried simply by the bolts. The recess traps moisture which can lead to decay.

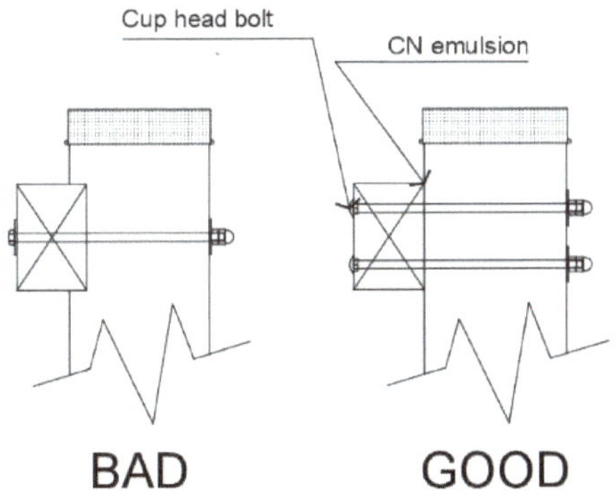

It is our opinion that housed joints should be avoided. Examples of good and bad connections are shown in Figure 94. The good connection shows how a member is simply connected to the post with two bolts without any housing into the post. A layer of CN emulsion is placed between the two items and any excess wiped off.

Figure 94.   Connecting timber

Figure 95.   Top fixed handrail has failed

Figure 96.   Rails should fasten from underneath

Handrails, guardrails and barriers are by their very nature expected to be safe, so attention needs to be given to their construction to ensure they are actually safe. When a rail sits on the top of a post, it is almost universal practice to fasten through the top of the rail into the end grain of the post. This allows moisture to enter and decay is likely to result (Figure 95) and the potential for injury is obvious. Instead of using top fixings, all the attachments should be from underneath as in Figure 96.

Figure 97. This handrail has a small gap between each piece and a sloping top

Figure 98. Screws in a straight line have split the post

A top mounted rail can be improved by having a small gap between each piece so moisture cannot enter the end grain and so over time set up an environment conducive to decay. What is critical is that the top sheds moisture. Both of these features of good design and construction practices are shown in Figure 97 but the angle across the handrail need not be as steep. A slope of 6 to 10 mm will suffice. When a rail is screw fastened to the face of a post, they must be fully predrilled and in a staggered alignment. The consequences of not doing this are shown in Figure 98.

Connecting round timber can be more difficult even with true dimension pine. Some low-cost brackets do exist, but we have never seen them in anything other than light gauge steel with light galvanising. The simplest way is probably to form a flat on both items and use a standard rectangular bracket. Connections that use a strap over the top as with a diamond configuration should not be used as the corners can be dangerous.

Identify Critical Areas

Figure 99. Critical zones must be identified

Some areas of your playground design will be more critical than others should there be a failure for whatever cause. The equipment envisaged in Figure 99 have two problem areas. While not strictly a free-standing structure it will be less rigid than hoped should there be a failure at groundline. Of more concern would be the member that attaches to the middle of horizontal post. This would normally be connected by a vertical bolt, but this will introduce moisture directly into the centre of the support. Alternatives would need to be considered, perhaps timber cleats with horizontal fixings or a U bolt if there is sufficient height. Better still, add another post.

Attaching Accessories

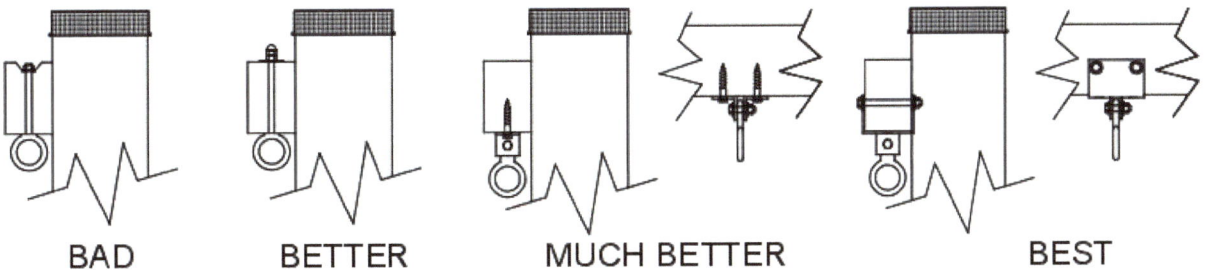

Figure 100. Different methods of attaching to a horizontal beam

Thought must be given to adopting the best method of attachment of equipment such as swings or ropes etc. to the timber to minimise and degrade over time. Figure 100 shows four means which are described as bad, better, much better and best. The reasons for categorising them this way is:

Bad: The bolt is vertical and has been countersunk to ensure there is no protruding thread. Any moisture is funnelled directly down into the centre of the timber member and so bringing with it the potential for decay. It is only a single bolt with no redundancy should it fail.

Better: The top of the timber is not recessed so less moisture enters the centre, so the likelihood of decay is reduced but not eliminated. It is only a single bolt with no redundancy should it fail.

Much better: By using coachscrews from underneath there is no chance of moisture entering. The screws will be in a straight line though and there is a chance of splitting the beam. 10 mm coachscrews particularly run the risk of being overstressed. Two fasteners are safer than one.

Figure 101. Through bolts allow moisture into the beam

Best: All bolting is horizontal so there is no chance of splitting if clearances are maintained. Two bolts are always safer than one. The required distance between the bolts and the edge of the beam needs to be maintained and better still, not be in the same alignment (Figure 102).

As has been discussed, fasteners should be stainless, as with any bracket.

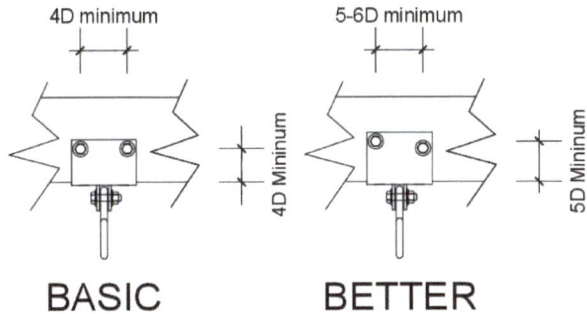

Figure 102. Basic and better arrangements for horizontal bolting.

Inspection of Fasteners

Figure 103.   The chain failed because it could not be inspected

Good design with fasteners will ensure that there can be easy inspection of the timber structures as well as all the ancillary equipment that is attached to them. As has been mentioned under post supports it is important that they extend above the undersurfacing and that the bolts be visible without the need for any excavation– compare Figure 54 with Figure 64 which shows how this can be achieved. The equipment itself should also be able to be inspected with similar ease. The bridge in Figure 103 was able to have its connections at each end inspected easily but the worn link in the conduit could not be inspected.

9 DOCUMENTATION AND CERTIFICATION

General

Ted has been asked to quote to supply timber against many playground drawings, some of which can be classed as little more than "thought bubbles". They have been singularly lacking in detail and specification. There is a place for this type of drawing but not when it is issued as "For Construction" as he has seen. Drawings which simply present an architectural intent should be marked as such and the notes must contain clear advice to the tenderers of all the documentation and certification, they must supply to fill in the missing gaps.

The NCC includes a Class 10b Structure which is described as "being a fence, mast, antenna, retaining or free-standing wall, swimming pool or the like." That definition does not specifically mention playgrounds but the wording "or the like" is an extremely broad brush bringing in almost anything imaginable. (Ted still cannot believe the battle he had trying to build a timber drying kiln and the local council building inspector was demanding he put windows and doors in it on the basis of "or the like.") Given that the landscape Industry is unregulated, and no doubt with its fair share of "cowboys" and the potential risks to the public and consequential litigation can be very high. it seems to both Ted and Ralph that it is unwise to engage in semantics. Rather, designers and asset owners should, and indeed must, fully embrace the need for a high degree of caution and full documentation including independent assessment of public playgrounds.[195]

When we were supplying bridges and boardwalks our consulting engineer fought against the generalists who certified subdivisions and the like. He argued that these structures did not come under the Class 10b Structure classification and required specialists to know what they were looking at and be able to assess them. Likewise, every aspect of a playground certification must be by specialists whose public indemnity specifically mentions "playground certification". He/she must in turn be checking that all professionals and contractors have the word 'playground" in conjunction with their involvement whether it be design, equipment, installation, or surfacing.

Minimum Documentation

The purchaser, asset owners and any occupants of the land on which the playground[196] is situated (termed the operator in the standard)[197] must maintain the following documents:

- Documents requiring the signed certification of an Engineer

---

[195] This chapter draws heavily from Consulting Coordination Australia's documentation. *Enhance Advisory - 0720 - Playground Compliance. Enhance Advisory - 0917 - What Needs Certification (Play, Fitness, Parkour, Skate). Version 3* and *Ensuring Compliance of Equipment (Play, Fitness, Parkour, Skate). Version 3* (Sydney: Consulting Coordination Australia. Varying dates).

[196] These guidelines should not be limited to children's playgrounds but apply to the range of associated facilities including adventure playgrounds, skate parks, childcare centres, waterparks and custom play spaces where the environment is part of the playspace.

[197] Standards Australia *AS 4685.0 -2017 Amd 1:2019 Playground equipment and surfacing, Part 0: Development, installation, inspection, maintenance and operation*. (Sydney: Stadards Australia.2019) Clasue 5.9.

- - Certificate of compliance to the version of AS4685 *Playground equipment and surfacing, Part 0: Development, installation, inspection, maintenance and operation* which is current at the time, and
  - Certificate of structural compliance to the NCC. (These two certifications may be single documents or combined into one.)

- Documents that require a signed Engineer's Certificate or NATA Certification prior to commissioning
  - Certificate of Compliance to the version of *AS4422 Playground surfacing - Specifications, requirements and test method* that is current at the time.

Before you Start

Before a designer puts pen to paper, they need to talk to their playground certifier. An engineer may design timber elements, but he/she will not certify the equipment that is attached to it as it could be outside of hie/her area of expertise. This means a specialist play safety engineer is especially important. The equipment manufacturer will certify his/her equipment but quite possibly only when it is part of their biscuit cutter playground and not a custom unit. The softfall installer will be very limited in what he can certify. As well, an otherwise compliant playground equipment may not be compliant considering where it is installed and adjacent elements. Your certifier has to bring all this together in a single certificate and he cannot be engaged as an afterthought. His/her experience with different providers and a whole of site vision can head off serious difficulties at the end of the project.

The Responsibilities of the Parties

Equipment designer

The equipment designer has a general duty of care to ensure that their products meet all the requirements of the standards and have specific playground equipment insurance. Ted and Ralph believe that a product specific timber specification must be used as opposed to just asking for house framing timber. Independent verification of timber grade compliance is also, in our opinion, a necessary requirement of the design. We would further advise that with any timber elements in the playground that the relevant sections of the design checklist which is part of this guide be completed.

Playground designer

The playground designer is responsible to assure that the accessibility code has been complied with and that the minimum fall zones designated by the equipment designer have been met. Specific playground equipment insurance is required. Similarly, independent verification that the timber is to grade should be nominated on the drawings. We would further advise that with any timber elements in the playground that the relevant sections of the design checklist which is part of this guide be completed.

Equipment Supplier

The "equipment supplier" is anyone supplying playground equipment in any form. He/she is responsible to ensure the required Engineer's certification is in place. If the supplier is also the installer it is necessary that the playground's certification is also obtained and provided. It is necessary that the insurance specifically mentions the supply of playground timber. They should be requiring and maintaining and also supply records of independent verification of the timber as being to grade. It is necessary that documentation containing the correct assembly, erection, placement information and also list any special tools. All of this along with the playground certification must be supplied in English. Other information that must be supplied is warranty information, foundation details, any special instructions, and instructions on painting and protective coatings.

The level of maintenance and inspection required from routine to comprehensive and annual must also be documented. It is necessary also to provide detailed equipment parts identification and the necessary information needed to order replacements.

Playground installer

The playground installer generally must ensure and document that the equipment is installed not only in accordance with the requirements playground safety standards but also that of "best practice". The manufacturer and the designer's recommendations may be different from those in this guide e.g., engaging with the ground or species choice, as we have focused on "best practice" not common practice. When there is a difference between this guide and the manufacturers recommendation, the installer must document his communication with the manufacturer seeking direction. The installer must carry the necessary insurance specifically mentioning the installation of playground timber.

When the supplier is also the installer it is, in Ted and Ralph's opinion, necessary to maintain and supply records of independent verification that the timber is to grade. This is alongside the certification usually supplied covering the equipment and installation of the whole playground.

Surfacing manufacturer/supplier

The surfacing manufacturer/supplier must supply the necessary signed Certification that the surfacing material has been tested and that it complies with the standard. The manufacturer must carry the necessary insurance requirements specifically mentioning the supply of playground surfacing.

Surfacing installer

Prior to commissioning, the surfacing manufacturer/supplier must supply the necessary signed Certification that the installed surfacing material meets the requirements of the equipment manufacturer and the surfacing manufacturer. The installer is not able to "self-certify" what is his own work. All wet-pour surfaces must be independently tested and certified for compliance with AS4422 by an engineer or NATA specialist. The surface installer must carry the necessary insurance requirements specifically mentioning the installation of playground surfacing.

Playground Certifier

The certification will be provided by an Engineer or Building Certifier relying on the certificates provided by the parties that have any involvement. It is necessary to ensure that the Certifier has the specialised knowledge to understand what he/she is looking at and assess if the actual total installation is compliant with relevant safety standards for playground. The insurance requirements can be onerous. As mentioned, he/she should have been engaged prior to design actually starting.

International Certification
There is provision in Australia under the Washington and Sydney Accords to recognise certification by an international Engineer from some countries but, at the time of writing, many imported playgrounds are from countries that are not included in the Accord.[198] The documentation must be in English! In the case of supply outside of the agreement the equipment must be certified from scratch. When the certification is from a country covered by the accord it is necessary to have an engineer registered in that state to countersign that it is suitable for local conditions, e.g., cyclone loadings, timber pests and footing details.[199]

Equipment Without Current Certification
When there is no certification available (lost or never completed) the duty of care on the owner of the property or anyone occupying it is to have the equipment Recertified. Owners or occupiers can be seen as negligent and so held liable if there is a claim in the absence of a Certificate of Compliance. When the equipment predates the present standard should have documentation from the date it was installed. Where the original certificate is present there is no legal obligation to update to the latest requirement. Inspection Certificates are to be obtained annually (refer to the chapter, *Maintenance and Inspection*).

---

[198] Refer to the Engineers Australia website for the current list.
[199] This requirement for recertification must not be taken lightly. Ted recalls being beaten on a footbridge quotation but when he saw the imported product, he realized it simply could not be right. Under Right to Information, he obtained the plans which were in German and they only had a few basic dimensions but no member or fastener sizes. The drawings appeared to have been simply rubber stamped by an Australian Engineer and a certificate issued that it had been designed to the steel structures code. It was made of aluminium and had serious safety issues!

10 INSPECTION AND MAINTENANCE

Frequency of Inspection

There are four levels of mandatory playground inspection,[200] Comprehensive post-installation, Routine, Operational and Comprehensive.[201] The person doing these inspections must be "competent" to do them and this competency can come through "training, qualifications or experience"[202] Courses are available for each of these levels which would normally cover the whole park facilities rather than just the playgrounds. There is no legislation requiring these inspections to be done by qualified people.[203]

At Installation: Before first opening to the public, a comprehensive inspection of the playground is undertaken by a competent (qualified?) person with the training and experience to confirm that the playground does meet the relevant areas of AS 4685 series and AS 4422. Any shortcomings are documented to ensure they are rectified before opening. If a non-conformance is found that is not an unacceptable risk to the users, the park may still open.[204] It is hoped that this guide will empower the inspector to understand what is entailed in a suitable timber installation.

Daily or Weekly: This very regular check is termed a *Routine Inspection* and is mandatory under AS 4685.0-2017. No specific time period between inspections is stipulated as this will depend on local conditions but it may be required daily and it would seem to be imprudent to go longer than a week. Though there is a Unit of Competency *AHCPGD206 - Conduct visual inspection of park facilities*, this task would normally fall into the duties of unqualified cleaning staff. In practical terms there is no need for specialised training as it simply looks for the obvious, such as vandalism, overhanging and dead branches, the depth of any softfall such as sand, damage and for anything that has been introduced such as broken glass or syringes.[205] Ted's observation is that this may be impractical for staff to have this formal qualification, especially in smaller local governments where staff turnover could be higher, and the level of inspection is so basic. This very low-level inspection is done by people who have limited autonomy and work under supervision and must be documented against an already prepared checklist.[206] Accordingly, it is our opinion that inspecting for timber issues, (apart from the glaringly obvious such as vandalism), will be outside of the ability of this inspector.

Every 1-3 months: The second level of mandatory inspection is the *Operational Inspection* and AS4685.0 says that a compelling reason is required for this to be longer than every three months.[207] This visual check looks at the operation and stability of the playground and associated facilities. The person doing the inspection should hold Unit of Competency *AHCPGD305 - Conduct operational inspection of park facilities*. Inspection at this stage is still via a checklist. Failure by the equipment owner/operator to complete this regular inspection by a competent, and better, competent and qualified person is considered

---

[200] This section of the chapter draws heavily from Consulting Coordination Australia's document. Enhance Advisory - 0917 - What Needs Certification (Play, Fitness, Parkour, Skate). Version 3 (Sydney: Consulting Coordination Australia. 2017).
[201] *AS 4685.0 -2017 Amd 1:2019*, Clause 8.5.1.
[202] *AS 4685.0 -2017 Amd 1:2019*, Clause 5.1. There appears to be a conflict in the standard as clause 8.7.2 requires training and experience where in 5.1 it is training or experience.
[203] Dodd, Lachlan. *Pers. Com.* 27 January 2021 as is also indicated in the relevant Unit of Competency course outlines.
[204] *AS 4685.0 -2017 Amd 1:2019*, Clause 8.5.2
[205] *AS 4685.0 -2017 Amd 1:2019*, Clause 8.5.3
[206] Australian Government. Unit of competency details *AHCPGD206 - Conduct visual inspection of park facilities (Release 1)*. Accessed January 27, 2921. https://training.gov.au/Training/Details/AHCPGD206.
[207] *AS 4685.0 -2017 Amd 1:2019*, Clause 8.5.4

a breach of duty of care and will not stand up to legal scrutiny in the event of an incident. A person undertaking this inspection is meant to be able to take responsibility for his own work and for the quality of the work of any subordinates. As timber issues develop slowly and the inspector's responsibilities greater,[208] it is Ted's (and Ralphs?) opinion that the critical need for qualified timber inspection starts only at the Operational Inspection stage.

This chapter will give some guidance in what to look for in timber related matters though it cannot be construed as a complete instruction. Areas inspected over and above the Routine Inspection include, but are not limited to wear of moving parts, checking the fasteners are tight and are not missing, protrusions and sharp edges, the structural adequacy and stability of the equipment, excessive corrosion, fraying ropes and cables and clearances.[209] Special attention is to be given to single fasteners.

At least annually: The highest level of mandatory inspection is the *Comprehensive Inspection* which is required on at least an annual basis. Its purpose is to establish the overall level of safety of the equipment, foundations, and playground surfaces.[210] Impact attenuating surfaces must be tested at least every three years.[211] It may be undertaken by staff of the asset owner or by a maintenance contractor. Even at this stage there is no requirement or even a framework for the inspector to be licenced, just that they be trained and have experience.[212] It would be very unwise to engage an inspector who does not hold the Unit of Competency *AHCPGD505 - Conduct comprehensive inspection of park facilities as* the required level of expertise is much higher. The inspector must possess a deep knowledge in a range of advanced skills, be able to analyse information and exercise judgement in this specific technical area. Rather than just identify problems they must be able to offer solutions to them. They have accountability for their own work and the work of others. Rather than work to a checklist they work to the range of Australian Standards that are applicable, government legislation including access and workplace safety as well as manufacturer's standards[213] combined with their understanding of best practice.[214]

The timber inspection will be more through at the Comprehensive Inspection and some inspectors will not have the confidence to do this and may wish, initially, to engage a consultant with specialised knowledge.

---

[208] Australian Government. n.d. *Unit of competencey details - AHCPGD305 - Conduct operational inspection of park facilities (Release 1)*. Accessed January 27, 2021. https://training.gov.au/Training/Details/AHCPGD305.
[209] AS 4685.0 -2017 Amd 1:2019, Clause 8.5.4.
[210] AS 4685.0 -2017 Amd 1:2019, Clause 8.5.5
[211] AS 4685.0 -2017 Amd 1:2019, Clause 8.5.6
[212] AS 4685.0 -2017 Amd 1:2019, Clause 8.5.7
[213] Australian Government. *Unit of competency details - AHCPGD505 - Conduct comprehensive inspection of park facilities (Release 1)*. Accessed January 27, 2021. https://training.gov.au/Training/Details/AHCPGD505.
[214] Consulting Coordination. *Enhance Advisory - 0917 …*, 2

Inspection of Timber Playgrounds
General and tools required

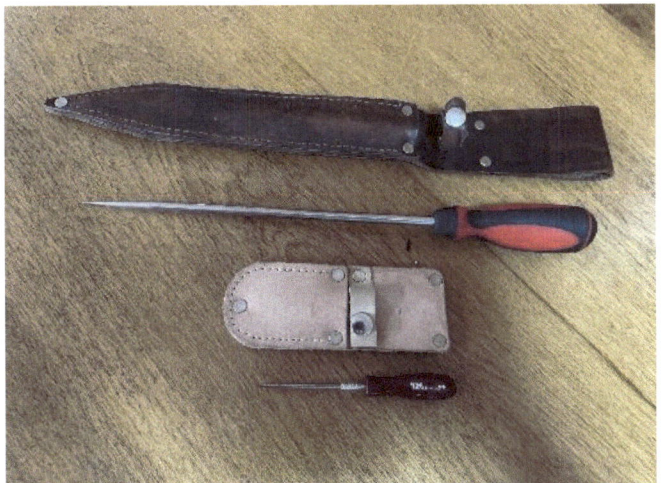

Figure 104.   Probes to check for decay

Figure 105.   Detecting decay at groundline

The main concern with timber playgrounds is decay. There is a remote possibility that decay will be present in the timber at the time of installation and unless it is only surface and slight such timber should have been discarded prior to installation. An inspector may encounter decay at:

- Groundline
- Where two members touch, and
- At the fasteners.

Generally, the appearance of the timber changes when decay is present making the inspector's task easier, but it can be confirmed simply by probing with a very sharp spike. Ted uses two commercially available probes from O ring removal tool kits. One is large for general work and the other which is smaller and is used to check between decking boards. These are extremely sharp and must be kept in a scabbard. A set of digital vernier callipers make accurate and quick measurement of end splits and longitudinal cracking while a tape measure will also be needed to measure some defects. A moisture metre will not be needed.

Areas to Inspect

The following areas of inspection are not a complete list.

Species

There is the requirement under *AS4685.1-2021* that the timber used be at least durability Class 1 or 2 in-ground or above-ground. We have argued that this is too broad and needs generally to be durability Class 1. The inspection should confirm the durability ratings of the timber used to determine if they are fit for purpose. It is the opinion of Ted and Ralph that structures made from lower durability timber[215] should

---

[215] E.g., refer to the comments made about kwila/merbau, robinia, larch and meranti in the chapter, *Standards and Fitness for Purpose*. Similar comments can be made about many Australian species.

not, indeed cannot, be granted a certificate.

Determining the species used is a very imprecise art and, if uncertain, the inspector may need to refer to the original plans or seek a certificate from the supplier. If the inspector is reasonably certain what the species, his/her assessment can be supported by the burning splinter test.[216]

Decay at groundline

Figure 106.   Inspecting a timber post at groundline with a probe

Figure 107.   The same post cut 65-100 mm above groundline

Both steel and timber are prone to attack at groundline. It is always likely to be the area of greatest concern. When probing for decay it is important to test right at groundline. It is expected that the softfall will cause the environment around the base of the timber to be moister and so be prone to decay. This decay can quickly disappear once the inspector probes further up the length as Figure 107 shows. That particular ironbark post had been in the ground 50 years without any maintenance other than a couple of coats of oil.

Termite attack

---

[216] E.g., if a matchstick size piece of spotted gum is burnt it leaves a complete white ash. The timber species notes of the Queensland Department of Agriculture and Fisheries include the burnt splinter test.

Figure 108. Termite attack (prior to milling)

Figure 109. Termite mud bridge

Structural timber is generally allowed to have some termite damage provided it is slight and only on the surface so its extent can be fully assessed. Obviously, there should be no active termites. The piece of decking in Figure 108 has termite attack which is so severe that the screw has countersunk deeply into the timber. This is unsuitable for any use, especially playgrounds. The first line of defence is to have only used termite resistant timber for ground contact, and when not termite resistant the posts should be in steel stirrups. When stirrups are used, termite activity can be identified by the presence of mud bridges (Figure 109) connecting the timber to the ground.

If any termite attack cannot be determined to be only surface and slight, all the affected pieces must be condemned and replaced.

Sharp points

Figure 110. Star check in a tight knot

Figure 111. Shelling out

The inspection will need to look for sharp points that can at best catch clothing and at worse injure a child. Particular areas for inspection are:

- Shelling out, this is a delamination in the growth rings and can raise some very sharp grain
- The intersection of a gum vein on an edge and a face (Figure 29), and
- Tight knots developing a star check

Finger entrapment associated with splits

When it comes to fitness for purpose, we find ourselves disagreeing with the *AS4685.1-2021* assessment of when a split becomes a finger entrapment. The requirements are written around preventing a child breaking, degloving or even losing a finger as a result of becoming trapped during a "forced movement" such as sliding and swinging. (It should be noted that toe entrapment is also a very possibility.) A "forced movement" under the standard is something that is set up by a piece of equipment not a fall or walking along a balance log.[217] In addition to "forced movement" Ted and Ralph would add to this the rough and tumble of play with associated falls etc., that at least they knew when young since falls can increase the danger of any split.[218] In a timber playground, the risks from entrapment can come from holes and joins between timber members but the greatest risk will be from splits in the timber. Splits can occur on all faces i.e., top, sides and underneath and all alignments, vertical, horizontal, or angled, not just the top of horizontal pieces. They can also occur on the ends or longitudinally and not intersecting the end. End splits can prove the greater risk than those that are longitudinal, but the others are not without risk. Splits on vertical timber is a particular risk as "the fall 'motion' of the child is down and the finger can move in that same movement as the body into or along a split."[219] As one inspector commented, "If I were signing off the play space, I wouldn't accept that risk"[220]

The 2021 version of AS 4685 introduced a new clause about what entailed finger entrapment in splits which gave them the green light saying, "Splits in single pieces of wood shall not be considered finger entrapment where the gap diminishes towards the centre of the wooden part."[221] We consider this an imprudent relaxation if for no other reason than it lowers the bar for timber designer's mastery of their profession. Splits can be all but eliminated when the designer adopts best practice in material selection and detailing. As has been explained in the chapter dealing with round timber, end splits can be eliminated or at the very least minimised through selecting timber of low shrinkage, and of suitable diameter and incorporating anti split-plates and caps.

When splits are present and may present a finger entrapment (from 8 mm) or be in the process of opening up to the extent they are likely to become a finger entrapment they should be filled with a non-pick polyurethane filler.[222] It is suggested that filling commences at 5-6 mm,[223] before any potential finger entrapments do eventuate. If filled the sealant needs to be applied for the whole length.

Note: Fillers in low or doubtful durability timber such as larch and robinia can promote decay between the filler and the timber.

Splinters
Any splinters must be removed

Longitudinal splits
Splits may need to have the edges arrised.

---

[217] Robbe, Fiona. *Pers. Com.* 18 December 2020. Refer to AS 4685-2021, 4.2.7.6.
[218] Refer to the comments by Richter Spielgerate that see top splits as being the primary risk.
[219] Thomas, Greg. *Pers. Com.* 16 December 2020.
[220] Thomas, Greg. *Pers. Com.* 16 December 2020.
[221] AS 4685-2021, 4.2.7.6.
[222] Ralph has had success with Bostik Simson elastic sealant ISR 70-03.
[223] Dodd, Lachlan. *Pers. Com.* 21 January 2021.

Fasteners

Because any timber over 50 mm thick will be unseasoned, there will be some shrinkage and so fasteners will need to be retightened which should be part of the playground installers contract. Ideally this should be done just prior to or at the first annual inspection. The exception is when screws go directly from steel to timber where shrinkage is not an issue. Inspection will include deciding whether retightening is required and looking for any protruding thread after any previous re-tightening. Extra attention will need to be given to fasteners that go vertically through a member as this can introduce moisture into the centre of the timber and promote decay. Consider the following:

Galvanised fasteners. When used without a factory applied epoxy coating it will be necessary to check them for corrosion and this can only be done by removing a number of items. Ralph's experience is that the head can look sound but the shaft can be badly corroded.

Lock nuts: Ensure there is sufficient length on the bolts so that the locking portion of locknuts engage on the thread

Dome nuts. These often will not have sufficient depth to allow the bolt to be tightened without the bolt bottoming out in the nut. If they are used we would recommend that they be used primarily as a locknut in conjunction with a standard nut and protection any protruding thread. At retightening the excess thread may have to be trimmed to ensure there is clearance at the end of the dome nut.

Figure 112. Locknut not engaging with thread

Maintenance and Surface Finishes

The good news is that if you have followed this guide your maintenance expenses will be slight and limited mainly to surface coatings and they should be quite reasonable. If you have not followed them that could be an entirely different matter! The maintenance which follows the required safety inspections will centre around items such as the fasteners and items attached to the timber e.g., swings and ropes. In that regard, the maintenance requirements for a timber playground are much the same as one made from steel. The main difference will be in surface finishes.

Preservatives.

The opportunity of preserving the timber has long passed after the playground has been installed and supplementary timber coatings do not necessarily improve the timber's resistance to decay. To Ted's knowledge there is only one paint-on "preservative" that is approved by the APVMA and that is copper naphthenate (CN) which is available in either an oil or a grease. These products are not suitable for skin contact.

Finishes, general

Weather exposure leads to the degradation of the timber surfaces, whether it is through UV effects or water absorption. Checking, cracking, delaminating, discoloration, twisting and bowing can be minimised by choosing durable timber and caring for your playground. There is a general understanding that timber should be "finished" but what does that term entail? There are three ways that people attempt to finish their timber, through penetrating oils, clear coatings and paint. The distinction between a penetrating oil and a clear coating isn't always understood. The way it is used in this book is:

- A penetrating oil soaks into the timber. It can provide a gloss to the outside of the timber for a time but its purpose is to be a water repellent and UV blocker.
- A clear coating is one that sits on the surface of the timber and sets in the same way as an opaque coating such as a paint sits on the surface of the timber.

Paint and clear coatings can, in fact, substantially increase the risk of decay under the surface as they can reduce the ability of the timber to dry out, particularly if the coating is cracked or flaking. Surface coatings do, however, minimise weathering and the potential for fungal organisms to develop on the surface if there is any moisture present. A structure such as a boardwalk can have a long service life without any finishes. However, the end sections of the members are much larger than we would normally use for a playground. It is important to consider whether a coating system, i.e., a clear finish, a clear coating or paint should be used at the time of construction and during its ongoing maintenance. But before discussing coatings, the related matter of leaching must be considered.

Leaching of Tannins

All Australian hardwoods leach tannins, as do most imported rainforest timbers and kiln drying hardwood does not remove tannin, only leaching does. The issue of tannin bleed has to be considered closely in most timber designs and while the situation is not as urgent for playgrounds, it still must be considered. It matters little if tannin drips into the softfall such as sand, but expensive coloured softfall surfaces are likely to stain. Some species, like kwila/merbau and blackbutt produce large amounts of extractives while on the other end of the scale, spotted gum probably produces the least. This is another good reason for choosing this species.

Figure 113. Leaching of tannins from recycled blackbutt

Even when the timber is "sealed" tannin can still be an issue. Three coats of a high-quality decking oil will not prevent leaching, even on spotted gum. Oiling unseasoned timber, which anything above 50 mm has to be, is not as successful as would be hoped. The oil simply cannot penetrate when the timber is still filled with moisture. Film finishes can even degrade from the inside out due to the effect of the extractives.[224] One manufacturer requires a four-to-six-week weathering period prior to applying their coating or having the timber pre-leached.[225] By leaving an extended period of time between installation and finishing, you will expect to have a problem from leaching if it rains over this period and it makes sealing all around impossible in some applications. Best practice in sealing requires the timber be coated all around, not just the visible face.

Specifying recycled timber **does not prevent leaching**. The timber may have been in service for 100 years but, as it is normally cut from larger sections such as girders, it will behave exactly the same as green off saw timber. It will generally not be seasoned and will leach in the same way. One way of dealing with leaching is to ensure the tannins drip onto gardens or grass where it will not matter. Another way is to pre-leach using proprietary products and these can be very effective.[226] It does not totally remove the possibility of leaching, but it does make it more manageable. When timber has been pre-leached it is more able to receive penetrating oils. The oxalic acid based proprietary products used to leach timber will also effectively remove tannin stains from concrete.

Figure 114. Pre-leaching timber

Paint

Before starting our discussion on paint, it should be noted that, based his experience, Ralph has serious misgivings about using it. He recounted how he had specified LVL rafters which extended past the house which were coated with a water-based paint. They were to have a glass roof over them protecting them from the elements. Unknown to him the client deleted this covering as funds were short and as a consequence the LVL's "wet rotted" under the paint. The paint manufacturer replied that some water-based paints were "pervious" i.e., that they let water through to the timber, trapping it and not letting the moisture escape. His strong preference is for a clear finish.

Figure 115. Appropriate paint can be a suitable product to use in a playground

Notwithstanding, if you proceed with an abundance of caution, the use of paint should not be discounted

---

[224] Damien McTague, Woodmans Timber Finishes. *Pers. Com.* April 19, 2001.
[225] Intergrain. *Dimension 4 Ultra Primer*. URL: http://www.intergrain.com.au/consumer/products/exterior/product-details/2744. Date accessed. June 15.
[226] Ted has had success using Intergrain *PowerPrep* followed by Intergrain *Reviva*.

as a playground finish. It should not be thought of only as a cheap alternative to using painted steel or aluminium. As one architect observed, "it still has a very timber look, . . . [and] always looks different to fibre cement or metal".[227] Paint, **provided the product has been well chosen**, is a very reasonable choice of finishes especially now that we can see manufacturers warranting their product for unheard of lengths of time. One manufacturer warrants residential paint for as long as the resident lives in the house while another mentions 100 seasons.

What is driving the longer service life in paint? As one paint chemist said, "They are finally pulling their head out of the sand regarding the variability of timber".[228] Considering the difficulties with timber, the following all impact on the success:

- high to low amounts of extractives,
- high to low pH,
- high to low shrinkage on unseasoned timber (13 to 3 %)
- continual dimension change with moisture content change,
- surface finishes from rough to smooth,
- high to low densities,
- backsawn or quartersawn,
- great variability in absorption
- great variability in grain characteristics, and
- Painting a dark colour over an existing light base

The wonder is that paint succeeds at all with the stresses this variability can impose! That is without the added stress on the timber caused by using a dark colour paint such as charcoal which absorb more of the sun's heat than light colours

Generally, the construction or maintenance team cannot go wrong if they follow the manufacturer's recommendations, but Ted is not so sure that is always the case with paint. Some time ago, he built a truss bridge with painted 50x38 mm unseasoned balustrades, he had the local sheltered workshop paint them and they used a premium acrylic gloss over a water-based primer as was instructed on the can. The workshop left them on a rack for a few days and then stacked them to return to our site. They all glued together and, when separated, tore off paint. Ted called the representative of that paint company and who said that he used the wrong primer. Notwithstanding what was written on the can, an oil-based primer should have been used. So much for labels. Even now we could be excused for being a little confused when determining the correct primer as different manufacturers specify differently. In Table 18, Ted gives in summary form the recommendations of four different paint manufacturers for primers under external acrylic paint.

---

[227] Mainwaring, John. *Pers. Com.* April 27, 2015
[228] Ted's source would rather not be named.

Dulux Weathershield Gloss	Wattyl Solagard Ultra-Premium Low sheen	Taubmans Sunproof Exterior	Accent Solarmax
Self-priming on timber[229] (3 coats required)	"If painting with white & white tone colours on a tannin rich timber, apply an initial coat of Solagard® as a sealer"[230]	"Tannin rich timbers should be primed with Taubmans Prep Right Wood Primer or Taubmans 3 in 1."[231]	"Where a primer is not specified apply three coats to previously unpainted surfaces"[232]
Table 18.	Different priming instructions for acrylic paints.		

This unfortunate experience with adhering from block stacking, though reduced next time around, was not totally solved by changing to an oil-based primer. (The issue was block stacking, not primers, and is something you need to consider if you are specifying a painted finish). The flexibility and permeability of the paint needed to withstand the variability of paint is exactly the reason the timber glued together. But what is the right primer, water, oil or no primer at all? Regardless of the recommendations above, all these manufacturers manufacture a primer suitable for these paints and what are we to make of a comment suggesting a primer "may" or "should" be specified?

A primer is used to provide a strong bond between the wood and succeeding coats. It functions as a sealer and a water repellent, sometimes with fungicides added and is formulated to have a dull finish and so aid with the adhesion of the topcoats. When Ted first started selling paint, the sales representative told him, "Oil and water do not mix, so do not use an oil primer under a water-based topcoat". It sounds logical but it was incorrect as oil-based primers are frequently used under water-based paints. (Going the other way, water-based primer to oil-based topcoat is a problem though) Timber Queensland is more specific in their advice relating to cladding which is similar to playgrounds in the terms of risk. They say, "For all cladding where a painted finish is required, boards **should** (emphasis mine) be **primed all round** (emphasis mine) with a solvent (oil) based primer plus one coat of undercoat, colour matched to the final finishing coat. This will ensure that significant colour variations will not be apparent due to any shrinkage or movement that may occur later. Knots should be sealed with a two-pack polyurethane or other sealer recommended by the paint manufacturer" to prevent resin bleed through the paint.[233] (This is particularly evident in pine chamferboards for instance.) A primer, most likely oil based, should be part of your paint specification.

What type of paint should you use? In 2006 Timber Queensland advised, "Solvent borne (alkyd or oil) finishes are more resistant to water vapour than water borne (acrylic) finishes. Where a high level of protection is required, a finish system with a solvent borne primer and/or undercoat should be selected". While acknowledging the easier application and the improvements in water-based paints, the objection was that "softer films tend to retain more dirt than alkyd (solvent based) paints, and thus harbour more

---

[229] Dulux. *Dulux Weathershield Gloss Datasheet*. URL: http://www.duspec.com.au/duspec/file/AUDD0054.pdf. Date accessed. January 31, 2021.

[230] Wattyl. *Wattyl Solagard Ultra Premium Low Sheen. Data Sheet*. URL http://services.valsparprofessional.com.au/uploads/tds/D4.14%20-%20Solagard%20Low%20Sheen.pdf. Date accessed. January 31, 2021.

[231] Taubmans. *Sunproof*. URL. http://www.taubmans.com.au/Paints/Sun-Proof. Date accessed. 31 January 2021.

[232] The instructions on the *Accents Solarmax* can. Date viewed July 17, 2015

[233] Timber Queensland *Technical Datasheet 5, Cypress and Hardwood Cladding*. (Brisbane: Self Published, 2014), 1. Bootle is less definitive with the term "often used". *Wood …*, 151.

mould growth".[234] Despite advances in paint technology, they saw no reason to revise that recommendation in the March 2014 review of their recommendations. Against this there are now water-based enamels that are promising, at least through accelerated weathering trials, to match the performance of the premium acrylics. There can be no substitute for obtaining a written recommendation for a primer and topcoat from reputable paint suppliers especially when new formulations are being released.

A successful painted playground project will include the following:

- a light colour should be chosen to extend the life of the paint and timber,
- there will be no housed joints,
- Ideally all joints should be painted before assembly,
- the ends will be sealed,
- the primer will be checked for adhesion if factory applied, and
- the topcoat will be applied by brush.[235]

If you want paint to succeed, there are two critical things above the five points mentioned above you must do. These are:

- Have a site-specific recommendation from a paint manufacturer
- It is advisable to count the number of coats that are applied or follow the recommended micron thickness of the paint film coats being applied and,
- Have no more than 29% solids when the dimension is over 50 mm.[236]

Clear coatings

Even more care needs to be taken when considering whether to use a clear coating on playgrounds than any other alternative. These films can easily be the "maintenance nightmare." Many professionals have reported very disappointing results to both Ted and Ralph and consequently a reluctance to use them. This is something we have also observed on many projects and experienced firsthand. One researcher noted "the performance of clear coatings on wood has generally been so poor that they are not recommended for finishing of exterior woodwork unless regular and costly maintenance is carried out."[237] Film finishes have to deal with the same variability as mentioned under the *Paint* section above which cause many of the problems but not all.

Figure 116.   Film finishes can be very high maintenance.

UV Blockers are a critical component of clear coating finishes and opaque paint coatings. The coating

---

[234] Timber Queensland. *Technical Datasheet 2, Finishes for Exterior Timber*. (Brisbane: Self Published, 2014), 1.
[235] Paints are formulated so that when applied with a brush without any thinning, the correct paint thickness is applied.
[236] This point is stressed in the bridge inspection courses taught by Dr Dan Tingley of Wood Research and Development.
[237] Evans Philip D. et al.. 2015. "The Search for Durable Exterior Clear Coatings for Wood." *Coatings*. 831.

should contain blockers that protect the timber and different blockers that protect the film itself. These blockers are expensive, and some low-priced finishes have neither! Without the blockers that protect the timber, the fibres start to break down into a fine powder, indiscernible to the naked eye. Once this happens you have a member that is, in effect, wrapped in cling film. The microclimate between the wood and the film can then hasten decay. Any break in the film, which can be caused by natural feature, unsealed butt joints, or fasteners or wear and tear in the playground can also allow moisture to enter and promote decay. As mentioned under the Leaching section above, the extractives themselves can cause the film to breakdown from the inside out. This is why, with hardwoods, most clear coating manufacturers recommend a leaching period of something like six to eight weeks. But remember, in our drought prone land, if it has not rained, which it might well not have done over an eight-week period, it has not leached so you may have to introduce washing as part of the coating plan. Do not expect recycled timber to be pre-leached. The finish should also be of a thick consistency so forcing the painter to put on a heavy coat by brush.[238]

Figure 117.   CN oil on deck and clear coating on battens.

Figure 118.   Decay in spotted gum under a premium film finish after eighteen months.

Figure 119.   **Film finish on spotted gum battens.**[239]

Figure 120.   Film breaking down after six months

---

[238] Ted is aware of one project in north Queensland where the painter applied three thin coats and after an expensive claim the manufacturer reformulated the finish so it could not be applied thinly.
[239] This fence is a good example of the use of sawmill recovery sizes.

The Achilles heel of film finishes is maintenance. If the film is left to deteriorate it will need to be completely sanded back to bare timber between coats. This means that frequently (if not eventually mostly) recoating simply is not done. If it is recoated, and it will need to be done on a very regular basis, it will be a costly exercise. These finishes can be used over rough sawn timber but it is necessary to sand before the first coat otherwise a very rough finish results. Manufacturer's recommendations can include a further sand between subsequent coats. Under no circumstances use steel wool to sand as rust marks can develop on the timber.

Penetrating Oils

Not all penetrating oils are clear. There is little doubt that the most robust penetrating oil that can be applied is CN oil (refer to the decking in Figure 117 which is coated in CN Oil). The abbreviation CN stands for copper naphthenate. Against CN's superior performance is the fact that it should not be in contact with bare skin so it is unsuitable for playgrounds and it definitely is not "clear". CN oil has approval as a preservative but needs reapplication at least every seven years.

Figure 121. Freshly applied penetrating oil on ironbark.

If you are hoping for any oil other than CN to work as a preservative, you will be disappointed as they do not exist. If you have neither received the correct natural durability and/or treated the sapwood correctly you cannot make everything correct by using an oil, even an expensive one. At the time of writing there are no oils other than CN that can be claimed to be a preservative.[240] The main things you can expect from a penetrating oil is that it **works as a water repellent and a UV blocker**. The same thing can be said about UV blockers in penetrating oils as with clear coatings. They are expensive and some products can have very little of them, indeed they can have very little water repellency as well. Fortunately, unlike paint and clear coatings, penetrating oils are not affected by dimensional change.[241]

As mentioned, people can confuse clear penetrating oil finishes with clear coatings as, when the oils are first applied, it does have some level of gloss finish, but this is frequently short-lived, especially on unseasoned timber. That does not mean it is not present and not working. Throw water on the surface and you could well find that it is still repelling water. Once the surface stops repelling moisture it is time to re-apply a new coat. There is no need to sand back at all, simply wash off any dust and kill any mould if present and then re-apply. This simplicity and relatively low cost make maintenance more likely to be

---

[240] Ted was responsible for having one brand which was making this claim reported to the APVMA. If you hear anyone making this claim you need to check it with the APVMA.
[241] Bootle. *Wood…*, 146.

carried out.

How can you tell a good penetrating oil from one that is less so? Glossy cans and brochures and a high price are not necessarily a reliable guide and marketing claims should not be accepted on face value. Technical data sheets also don't necessarily show the relevant information required to determine a "good quality" product, the saying "oils ain't oils" stands true. A good quality oil should contain ingredients like:

- Resin system or oil suitable for timber. Often resins are modified to have characteristics which address limitations of natural oils. This can include mould growth in linseed oil and lanolin
- UV absorbers which offer protection to timber substrate and resin/oil system
- Water repellents. These can vary significantly in type and quality. It is good to have something that is not prone to mould e.g., linseed oil and lanolin seem to promote mould
- Mould and algae inhibitors. These will not remove or prevent mould from pre-infected timber, and
- Solvent carrier that aids in penetration of ingredients into timber.

On this last point, there are many types of solvent systems. Many clear finish formulations contain petroleum-based solvents of varying flash points and levels of aromatics as well as those which have surfactants to allow water to be incorporated. The best penetrating oils contain a petroleum based solvent system as it is more able to penetrate into the timber and less prone to facilitate movement of tannins to the surface. A product which incorporates a solvent with a high flashpoint and low aromatics would be preferable. What does this mean? A high flashpoint (>60.5 deg C) will mean the product will not be considered flammable thus reducing risks for transport, storage and use. A low aromatic solvent will reduce odour and risk often associated with using solvents. While these features do not necessarily add to the quality of a product, they do provide benefits which make oil based clear finishes more amenable to use and hence get the best result in timber.[242] If you are going to apply multiple coats over time, those oils containing copper should be avoided as this will tend to blacken the timber.

There is one other very important thing you should expect from a penetrating oil. While it is not totally relevant to the subject of new playgrounds, it is very relevant when considering older equipment. This subject is the ability of the finish to seal CCA into the timber and so alleviate any concerns about touching them. It may also be a consideration if recycled power poles are used as these will be CCA treated (refer Figure 22).

Lanolin Based Oils

Lanolin based products are sometimes chosen as they are perceived as being the environmentally friendly answer but, with the wool grease content possibly as low as 10%, and the petroleum-based solvents at more than 60%, it is arguable if this is, in fact, the case.[243] It is probably no better or no worse than any other oil in this regard. This is a totally different issue to whether this particular finish works well or not.

---

[242] All of these points were considered in the development of Tanacoat. When you are considering specifying a penetrating oil you need to ask probing questions of the manufacturer to ensure you are asking for a product that is at least equal of Tanacoat.

[243] Lanoteck. *Lanotec Timber Seal Material Safety Data Sheet*. URL: https://www.lanotec.com.au/wp-content/uploads/SDS-Timber-Seal-Sep-2017.pdf. Date accessed. June 22, 2015.

Again, we can find unsubstantiated claims of preservation from this type of product.[244] There is a long way from protecting the floors of shearing sheds under a roof to fully weather exposed applications. As briefly mentioned in the previous section, mould growth can be an issue and inhibitors are required to address it.

Painting Steel Supports - general

If you choose to paint/repaint any steel components, you must be careful in specifying the coating. The purpose of the coating has to be clearly understood as some are purely decorative while others provide the primary and only means of corrosion resistance. Whatever topcoat is chosen, as with the timber finishes, it is important to obtain the manufacturers recommendations for preparation and priming which must be followed.

Decorative finishes

As has been mentioned, Ted once built a bridge once where the handrails were specified "galvanized and powder coated black" which is exactly what he did. It looked wonderful when first built and the coating was purely decorative, but he soon had a claim from his customer who was upset at the white blooming on the balustrades, (refer Figure 68). The application was not far from the sea and he quickly discovered that these situations needed a very expensive specialty powder coated finish. Having learnt a very costly lesson, he advises that designers seek a written site-specific specification from a reputable paint manufacturer as to the best process and product to use in a given location. Powder coating and other coatings over galvanizing has its own problems and some manufacturers don't recommend it.

Corrosion Resistant Finishes

A designer can achieve corrosion resistance equal to galvanized with a suitable paint, and even better resistance in a marine environment. Ted has found a two-coat epoxy siloxane system[245] excellent for these purposes but even then his practice was to put a sacrificial coating between the timber and the painted steel. This is to counteract the potential for corrosion from the extractives and natural acidity of the timber. Ralph has had good results from *Dulux Durebuild STE epoxy* combined with *Dulux Weathermax HBR polyurethane* topcoat. Consider how you can touch up the paint as it may get damaged during transit and erection and from vandalism. Consider, also how to maintain the steel during a major refurbishment after many years. Can it be re-coated in situ? It must also be able to be repaired with a paintbrush and not sent back to the paint shop as is the case with powder coating. A site-specific recommendation from a reputable supplier that meets these guidelines is essential.

---

[244] E.g., *Deck-doc*. URL: https://deckdoc.com.au/wp-content/uploads/2017/08/Deck-Doc-Difference.pdf. Date accessed. June 22. 2015. Ted easily found four other references to Lanolin being a preservative or reducing wood rot. His understanding at the time of writing is that no lanolin producer has had these claims verified.

[245] As Ted have been thanked by customers for introducing them to the product we use, He has no hesitation mentioning it here by name. The product Ted used was PPG's *PSX700* which is derived from a paint produced to withstand the marine environment and intense heat of rocket launches at NASA's Cape Canaveral. The two-coat system utilises an epoxy zinc rich primer (or other primers if required) for primary anti-corrosive protection, followed by the polysiloxane which also provides anticorrosive qualities as well as very high gloss, and long-term colour retention as required for topcoats. This system meets and exceeds the requirements of ISO 12944-6 C5-M High. This system provides corrosion protection to first maintenance of greater than fifteen+ years. When choosing a paint system, you should be specifying to ensure performance that matches this product.

11 CASE HISTORIES

Playground on the Broadwater, Southport, Queensland
Lesson, A workaround for H5 (CCA) Applications in Playgrounds

Figure 122.   Timber playground after 10 years in service

Figure 123.   These playground posts cannot be H5 with CCA. (H5 in ACQ is not readily available

During 2010, Ted worked with a playground designer and contractor building a playground on the Broadwater at Southport in Queensland. The posts were originally specified as H5 and while it is theoretically possible to supply in the newer preservatives, in practice it can even now only be met in hardwood and pine with CCA.

As H5 in CCA is not permitted when timber part of a children's playground, a "workaround" was necessary. Our "workaround" was to use durability Class 1 in-ground timber and measured the required diameter under the sapwood i.e., a 200mm H5 post became a 225mm iron bark post measured over the sapwood. The sapwood was treated to H3 with Tanalith E. (copper azole). The sapwood above ground will not degrade over its life span. Most likely, the sapwood in the ground will remain intact for a long time also but it does not matter if it does decay as it basically turns into soil during the process, and the posts remain tight.

When used on natural round hardwood, copper azole loses its chemical colour fairly quickly and appears untreated. CCA would have retained its green colouring for its whole life. Ted inspected the playground in 2017 and the condition was excellent.

Figure 124. Ralph Bailey inspecting posts treated to H3 which are in excellent condition after 10 years

Because the timber was close to or even in the ground the framing is all durability Class 1 in-ground species which also have natural termite resistance. There was no evidence of decay even at the groundline or any termite attack when Ted and Ralph inspected the playground again in early 2021. All the timber is original and in remarkably good condition which is aided by the higher level of shading from the trees than would normally be seen. With the benefit of an extra 10 years of experience, the only thing we would change is not to have any checkouts in the posts and use straight side decking.

The only maintenance in ten years has been three applications of a tinted oil stain. The use of a stain extends the life of the oil by providing extra UV blockers.

Arab Dhow in Qatar
Lesson. Seasoned: framing timber is not playground timber

Figure 125.   Arab dhow fabricated in Brisbane from spotted gum

Ted saw his first Arab dhow in Dar-es-Salaam harbour in Tanzania back in 1970 and was amazed at how such small timber trading vessels could travel such large distances. It bought to mind images of Sinbad and his sailors. Later again he saw them up close at a boatyard in Jeddah in the early 80's so you could imagine Ted's complete surprise when he was contacted by UAP, who were building a dhow in Brisbane. This one was never going to float though, as it was to be installed in the playground at the National Museum of Qatar. While this is a playground, it could equally be described as public art.

Ted's help was sought because teak, a traditional timber for this application was not available in the sizes required so an Australian substitute was needed. He advised the use of spotted gum, a local boat building timber. Unfortunately, only structural timber, not appearance grade was available, and this playground needed the absolute best quality. Ted has been talking for years about the difference between the two applications and few listened however UAP grasped it immediately, but it meant that they had to overorder by 30 percent to obtain what they needed. A lower moisture content was required than what was stated in the upper range of the millers' specification. The mill was able to accommodate this. The spotted gum was supplied by a Queensland mill.

Figure 126.   Prefabrication underway in Brisbane.

Ted was used to dealing mainly with deck and house builders where the most sophisticated equipment being used is a power saw and drill and, shudder, a nail gun. Their manufacturing was in an entirely different league. Ted saw that they worked with artists across all parts of the creative process: from commissioning and curatorial services, concept generation and design development, right through to engineering, fabrication, and installation. Their public art is produced using the latest innovative processes. UAP can be contacted directly for more information on this remarkable playground.

Queen's Park, Ipswich
Lessons: Developing a theme that considers the past and prefabricating off site.

Figure 127.   Mining themed playground in 2005

Design and installation: Playworks,
Timber supply and prefabrication: Ted

Queen's Park, a large area in the centre of Ipswich, is the first park that was designated in Queensland (surveyed 1842). The area was heavily into mining, and when the playground was being developed, it was considered that a mining theme would be appropriate. While a biscuit cutter approach could have been used, this historically themed playground shows sensitivity to the city's past.

Like the playground in the first case history, the equipment here also used natural round treated hardwood but in this case most of the posts are not free standing and cannot fall over in the event of any decay at groundline. In this situation appropriately sized spotted gum would be very acceptable. The timber is again only treated to H3 but the diameter is measured under the sapwood. Handling such heavy pieces requires cranes and it is expensive and hard to do on site when builders are inexperienced with this type of construction. Normal drills and bits simply are too light. The tower and smaller items were all prefabricated at Ted's Gatton premises and shipped to site. The width of the legs was kept to a maximum of 3.55 metres so an escort vehicle was not needed and so it was able to be carried by their usual delivery driver.

Note: Confirm your State's regulation for maximum widths and overhang when moving equipment by road

Figure 128.   Swale drain

Figure 129.   Park entrance

Large section timber was also used for the entrance to the park and which continues the historic theme. The large posts, with water shedding tops, are free standing but being sawn there is no appreciable sapwood so the treatment is again just to H3 so the small amounts on the corner are stabilised. It is critical that timber used this way is not embedded in concrete. The swale drain bridge uses rough sawn face decking with an almost clear face. This ensures longevity and slip resistance,

Part of the playground was the creation of a derelict tank stand, a nod to the time when every home had its own tank. It serves no purpose other than reinforcing the theme. These posts should be in the highest durability timber as they are free standing. In hindsight, recreating the bearers and joists at the top would be an advantage as safety is increased.

Figure 130.   "Derelict" tank stand and flying fox termination

Ports North, Cairns
Lessons: Timber playgrounds can succeed in the tropics, The importance of a playground certifier

Figure 131.   Ports North playground in its high-profile setting

Architect: CA Architects
Engineers: Arup
Playground certifier: CCEP
Timber supply: Ted

The Far North Queensland Ports Corporation Limited, trading as Ports North, is a Queensland Government Owned Corporation responsible for the development and management of a number of ports in North Queensland. Its operations and facilities are vital to the economic development of the regional centres they service and the State's tourism and export performance, and none more so than the Cairns Cruise Liner Terminal.

When the decision was made to build a playground adjacent to the terminal and under a large fig tree which was a local landmark, it required a design solution that was world class befitting its internationally highly profile site and the natural beauty of the location. To prevent the aesthetics of the site being impacted adversely, it was determined that the site needed to be unfenced. Wisely, it was realised that because the site was in the tropics there could be no compromise in the quality of the material and the detailing. Construction was completed in 2012 and the playground has been an overwhelming success.

Figure 132. Playground under construction

The decks generally follow the advice in this guide for best practice in construction with 120x35 mm decking laid on 75 mm joists with 14# screws installed in a staggered alignment. Posts are installed in stainless steel stirrups and all the fasteners are stainless. The playground is shown during construction in Figure 132 and note the use of conventional fasteners, not tamper resistant.

Effective tamper resistance was planned though and achieved in a very cost-effective way by simply screwing timber blocks over the fasteners. The species used would have been one of those preferred by Ted in Table 7. The treatment is Tanalith E (copper azole) and this combination in association with good detailing has been successful. The asset owner reported that only two pieces of timber have been replaced in nine years and that the playground is still in excellent condition in 2021.

The costs associated with running this playground are much higher than would be expected over one sited in a suburban park and can be contributed to some extent to the high public use of the facilities. Ongoing maintenance and operational aspects of the location are challenging, and construction design should consider these factors. Asset owners contemplating similar playgrounds must ensure that the operational team and management have factored these costs into their budget.

The asset owner stressed the importance of having the playground certifier involved from the very beginning. His role in bringing the different professions and suppliers and trades together into a single certificate was critical.

Figure 133. Conventional fasteners have been made safe with a block of timber

APPENDIX 1. OBSERVATIONS ON POST SUPPORTS

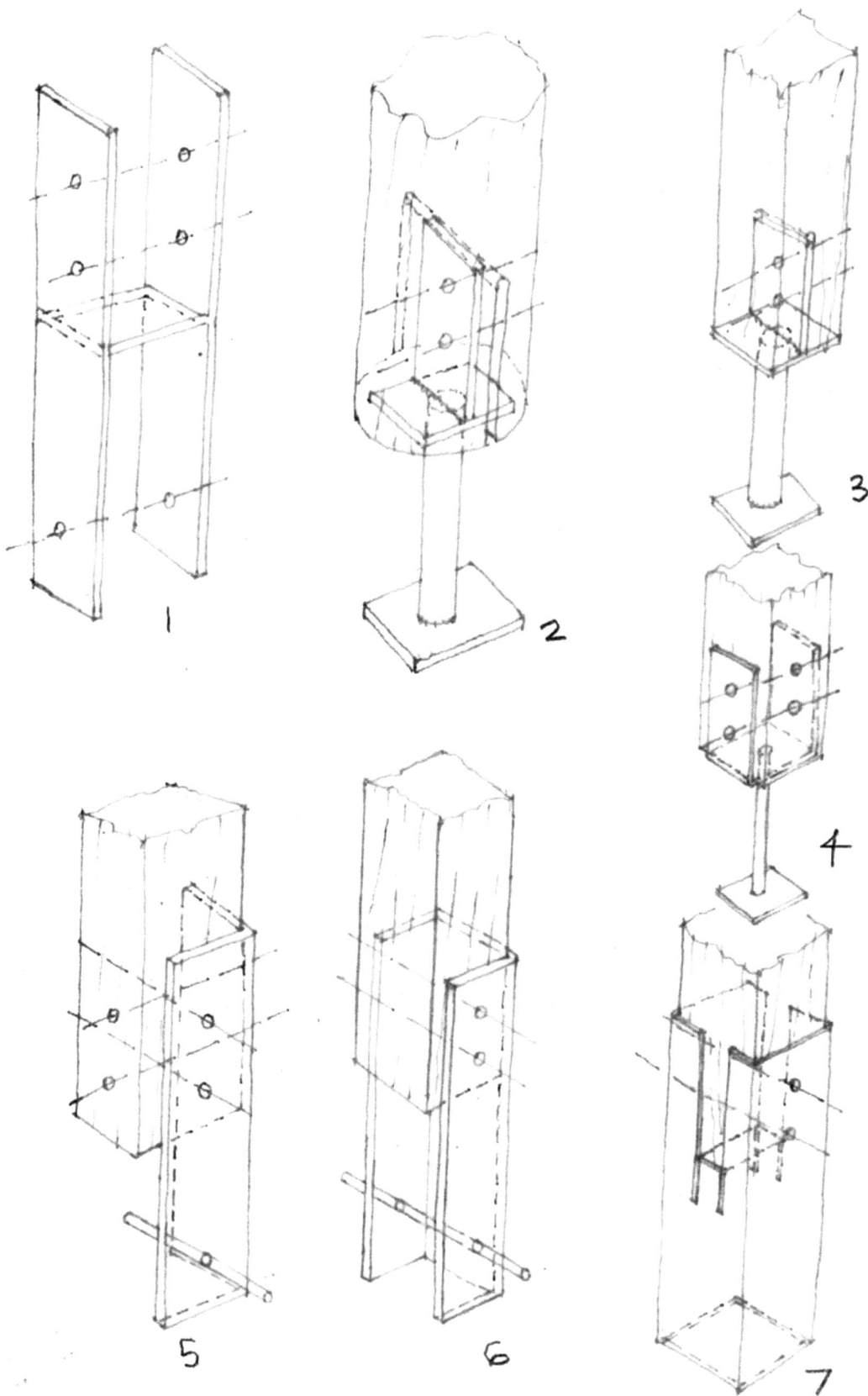

Figure 134. Different post supports encountered by Ralph

Drawing from his years of observations, Ralph has the following observations on the different post supports he has seen in his many years of experience. The numbers below match numbers shown in Figure 134.

1. Traditional "H" style post support has more stiffness than many "off the shelf" brackets but it does not accommodate shrinkage well
2. Vertical blade up the centre of a round post but there is normally only half the steel as in a "H" bracket to resist lateral movement. Commercially available brackets may be too light for playground use.
3. As with 2 above but shown on a sawn post
4. Low cost "off the shelf" post support in light gauge steel with inadequate connection to the footing
5. Rolled steel angle post support has no issues accommodating shrinkage
6. Rolled steel C section post support does not accommodate high shrinkage timber but is a good robust solution
7. Modified square hollow section is a creative solution but must be heavy gauge (at least 4 mm). Not suitable for high shrinkage timber

Note: Custom made post supports must be heavy gauge rolled steel, not light folded *Duragal* or *Supergal*. Ideally, they should be fabricated in stainless steel but, if not, painted to a site-specific recommendation as outlined in this book.

CHECK LIST

This checklist should not be considered as covering every situation in which timber is used in playgrounds but does contain general guidelines for making the correct design decisions. This checklist does not include inspection.

Item to check for	Circle which applies or comment
Timber Selection	
Note: there will be no perfect species and there will be some compromises in your selection.	
I am aware of the difference between sapwood, heartwood, and wood with heart	Yes No
I am designing primarily with	Hardwood Cypress Pine
The design decisions relating to heart are	
The design decisions relating to heartwood are	
The design decisions relating to sapwood are	
My timber is imported	Yes No
I have checked durability ratings with	AS5604 CTIQ[246] Bootle[247]
I am relying on overseas durability ratings and not checking Australian ratings for our climate	Yes No
If "Yes" I am aware that the ratings are different	Yes No
Preservative treatment is specified without CCA or creosote	Yes No
If using pine, have I requested that wax be added to the treatment	Yes No
All timber is durability Class 1 above-ground or in-ground as applicable	Yes No
I have noted that Ted and Ralph consider that H3 LOSP may not give satisfactory performance	Yes No
I have noted that Ted and Ralph consider that satisfactory treatment of sawn pine may not be achievable	Yes No

---

[246] CTIQ, Volumes 1 and 2.
[247] Bootle, K. *Wood in Australia.*

All sapwood is required to be treated	Yes No
If "No", why not	
I understand what Lyctus larvae are	Yes No
I understand that all sapwood is durability Class 4	Yes No
I have checked availability of the proposed timber	Yes No
Does my proposed timber have bushfire resistance	Yes No
Does my proposed timber have termite resistance	Yes No
My proposed species is one preferred by Ted and Ralph	Yes No
If "No", I have achieved the same outcome by	
My timber generally has interlocking grain	Yes No
The shrinkage of my timber is	
What might be the impact of this shrinkage rate	
Is the timber "greasy to the touch"	Yes No
I have referred to a species by all its botanical names and by its Standard Trade Names	Yes No
I have ensured that I have not referred to a local or marketing name	Yes No
Sawn Timber	
Have I said "kiln dried" without working through consequences	Yes No
The consequence for pine is	
The consequence for cypress is	
The consequence for hardwood up to 50 mm thick is	
The consequence for hardwood thicker than 50 mm is	
I am expecting recycled timber to be dry	Yes No
I am aware that Ted and Ralph warn against this expectation	Yes No
I will avoid CCA in recycled timber by	
I am aware of the issues with included heart in hardwood sizes 150x150 and smaller	Yes No

I am aware of the issues with included heart in hardwood sizes larger than 150x150	Yes No
Hardwood heart checks will be avoided by	
I am aware of durability issues relating to pine heartwood and heart	Yes No
I am aware of treatment issues relating to pine heartwood and heart	Yes No
I am aware that there will be insufficient sapwood on the hardwood to give durability and must rely primarily on natural durability	Yes No
I am aware that there must be 80% sapwood minimum in pine for preservation	Yes No
I am aware that in Ted's opinion preservation of pine is unlikely without incising	Yes No
I am aware that cypress sapwood cannot be treated successfully	Yes No
I am aware that Ted and Ralph warn that structural grades of timber may be unsuitable for playgrounds	Yes No
I am aware that Ted and Ralph recommend rough sawn sanded finish over dressed	Yes No
Why do they recommend this	
I have detailed the top of hardwood posts so they shed moisture or are capped	Yes No N/A
I have detailed caps for the top of cypress posts	Yes No N/A
I have detailed caps for the top of pine posts	Yes No N/A
Round Timber	
Am I aware of the potential for splitting heads and butts	Yes No
Have I capped the vertical posts	Yes No
If No" why not	
Have I pated and capped the horizontal posts	Yes No
If "No" why not	

Do my guidelines for capping follow Ted and Ralph's recommendations which include an anti-split plate	Yes No
If "No", I will achieve the same outcome by	
Are any round timbers separated by at least a 25 mm spacer	Yes No
If "No", I will achieve the same outcome by	
Timber Specifications	
Sawn timber	
I have followed Ted and Ralph's guidelines for hardwood sawn above-ground	Yes No
If "No", I will achieve the same outcome by	
I have followed Ted and Ralph's guidelines for hardwood sawn in-ground	Yes No
If "No", I will achieve the same outcome by	
I have followed Ted and Ralph's guidelines for hardwood kiln dried	Yes No
If "No", I will achieve the same outcome by	
I have followed Ted and Ralph's guidelines for hardwood unseasoned decking	Yes No
If "No", I will achieve the same outcome by	
I have followed Ted and Ralph's guidelines for cypress sawn all applications except decking	Yes No
If "No", I will achieve the same outcome by	
I have followed Ted and Ralph's guidelines for cypress decking	Yes No
If "No", I will achieve the same outcome by	
I have followed Ted and Ralph's guidelines for plantation pine above-ground sawn	Yes No
If "No", I will achieve the same outcome by	
I am aware that Ted and Ralph's do not recommend plantation pine decking	Yes No
I still choose to use it because	

I have followed Ted and Ralph's guidelines for plantation pine in-ground sawn self-supporting	Yes No
If "No", I will achieve the same outcome by	
I am aware that Ted and Ralph's do not recommend plantation pine for sawn free-standing applications	Yes No
I still choose to use it because	
I have required independent verification of grade	Yes No
If "No", I will achieve the same outcome by	
Natural rounds and parallel round pine	
I have followed Ted and Ralph's guidelines for hardwood natural rounds	Yes No
If "No", I will achieve the same outcome by	
I have followed Ted and Ralph's guidelines for cypress natural rounds in-ground self-supporting	Yes No
If "No", I will achieve the same outcome by	
I am aware that Ted and Ralph do not recommend cypress for free standing items	Yes No
I still choose to use it because	
I have followed Ted and Ralph's guidelines for plantation pine natural rounds above-ground	Yes No
If "No", I will achieve the same outcome by	
I have followed Ted and Ralph's guidelines for plantation pine natural rounds in-ground self-supporting	Yes No
If "No", I will achieve the same outcome by	
I am aware that Ted and Ralph do not recommend plantation pine for free standing items	Yes No
I still choose to use it because	
Engaging with the Ground	
My inground hazard zone	A B C D
Is there an increased risk because of the undersurfacing i.e., turf, softfall rubber, softfall bark chips	Yes No

Therefore, I will rate this as	A B C D
Do my embedded timber sizes match CTIQ	Yes No N/A
I am aware that Ted and Ralph do not recommend embedding timber posts in concrete	Yes No
I am following Ted and Ralph's guidelines for embedding posts	Yes No N/A
If "No", I will achieve the same outcome by	
I have specified the addition of a pole bandage	Yes No N/A
If "No" I will achieve extra life by	
I have chosen to use metal supports	Yes No N/A
How have I achieved two-way support	
Have I required stainless steel for my supports	Yes No N/A
Will my specification allow lightly galvanised "Duragal" style products	Yes No N/A
If "Yes", How will I achieve the same life as hot dipped galvanised	
Is my steel at least 4 mm thick if galvanised	Yes No N/A
If hot dipped galvanised, have I required additional anti corrosion paint	
Do I have a site-specific paint recommendation	Yes No N/A
Are my supports heavy black steel with corrosion resistant paint	Yes No N/A
Have I noted not to drill through the bracket	Yes No N/A
Do I have a site-specific paint recommendation	Yes No N/A
Do my supports have the potential for finger entrapment	Yes No N/A
Are all my fasteners above the undersurfacing and easily inspected	Yes No
Has an engineer determined the embedment depth	Yes No
Do my path terminations follow those of Ted and Ralph	Yes No N/A
If "No", I will achieve the same outcome by	

Fasteners	
Are my fasteners a minimum of 304 grade stainless	Yes No
If "No", I will achieve the same outcome by	
Have I avoided any coachscrews under 12 mm	Yes No
What level of vandal resistance am I aiming for	1 2 3
I have avoided overstressing of fasteners by	
Are fasteners in a staggered alignment along the grain	Yes No
If "No", I will avoid splitting by	
I am aware that predrilling will not always stop splitting along the grain	Yes No
Are screws at least 14 gauge (except in 19 mm decking)	Yes No
If "No", I am using lighter screws because	
Do my fasteners allow for retightening after shrinkage	Yes No
Do my fasteners allow for sanding of the deck surface	Yes No
If "No", my tightening procedure is	
Have I avoided any protruding bolts	Yes No
If "No", this is because	
Are my fasteners tamper resistant	Yes No
If "No", this is because	
Have I designed my fasteners for easy inspection e.g., none are buried/hidden	Yes No
Additional Construction Details	
Have I followed Ted and Ralph's recommendations for face fixing decking	Yes No N/A
If "No", I will achieve the same outcome by	
Have I followed Ted and Ralph's recommendations for fastening decking from underneath	Yes No N/A
If "No", I will achieve the same outcome by	
Have I avoided mitres in any decking	Yes No N/A

If "No", I will avoid sharp points by	
Are my corners pencil rounded, not arrised	Yes No
If "No", I will achieve the same outcome by	
Have I end sealed my timber	Yes No
If "No", why not	
Have I maintained all clearances on bolts and screws	Yes No
If "No", why not	
Have I avoided housed joints	Yes No
If "No", why not	
Is my bolting horizontal	Yes No
If "No", why not	
Have I identified critical areas	Yes No
If "No", why not	
Have I followed Ted and Ralph's guidelines for fastening accessories/	Yes No
If "No", why not	
Do I have rails sitting on top of posts	Yes No
Have I detailed fastening from underneath	Yes No N/A
If "No", why not	
Do I have rails fastened to the side of posts	Yes No
Have I detailed the screw in a staggered alignment	Yes No N/A
If "No", why not	
Do all rails shed moisture?	Yes No N/A
If "No", why not	
Surface Coatings	
I plan to use	Paint Clear finish, Clear coating finish, None at all
I have a site-specific coating recommendation	Yes No N/A
If "No", why not	

I have a site-specific penetrating oil recommendation	Yes No N/A
If "No", why not	
I am aware that Ted and Ralph do not recommend clear film finishes	Yes No N/A
If "No", why not	
I have prepared maintenance guidelines and timeframes for the playground owner	Yes No N/A
If "No", why not	
Certification	
Who have I have engaged to certify this playground	
Has the certifier bee engaged from the very beginning	Yes No
Does he have a copy of this guide	
If "No", why not	

SOURCE OF IMAGES

Images not acknowledged in this table are either from Ted Stubbersfield or the copyright holder has asked not to be acknowledged.

Figure 1	Old timber playground	Believed to be public domain
Figure 3	End section of a pine log	Shutterstock
Figure 8	Incised Pine	Tweddle Engineering
Figure 10	Lyctus attack	Trevor Smith, South Coast Home check
Figure 11	Lyctus attack	
Figure 12	Lyctus larvae	Doug Howick
Figure 13	Vandalism by fire	Copyright unknown
Figure 15	Free standing playground equipment	Shutterstock
Figure 16	Grain of turpentine	Wood Solutions
Figure 17	Grain of Gympie messmate	
Figure 19	Larch playground	Playquip leisure Ltd
Figure 29	Gum vein intersecting an edge and face	CB Architectural Timbers
Figure 31	Robinia as delivered to site	Jeff Nelson
Figure 32	Robinia after weathering	
Figure 33	Polecat	Pryda – not cleared
Figure 35	Longitudinal Splitting in pine	Fiona Robbe
Figure 36	Longitudinal Splitting in pine	Fiona Robbe
Figure 41	Cartoon	Fiona Robbe
Figure 42	Leaching Trials	Lonza
Figure 43	Contact Trials	
Figure 44	Free standing timber	Playworks
Figure 45	Self-Supporting timber	
Figure 58	Custom tool for post support	Queensland Department of Agriculture and Fishery
Figure 59	Example of hole for post support	
Figure 63	Corrosion at groundline	Ralph Bailey
Figure 75	Level 1 vandal resistant fasteners	Sentinel Group https://www.sentinelgrp.com.au/
Figure 76	Level 2 vandal resistant fasteners	
Figure 77	Level 3 vandal resistant fasteners	
Figure 82	Missing barrel nuts	Ralph Bailey
Figure 83	Barrel nut connection to timber	
Figure 88	Dome headed nails	Ralph Bailey
Figure 109	Termite mud bridge	Queensland Department of Agriculture and Fishery
Figure 123	Playground at Southport	Contrast Construction
Figure 125	Arab Dhow	UAP

Figure 126	Arab Dhow under construction	
Figure 131	Location view of Cairns playground	Ports North
Figure 132	Cairns playground under construction	
Figure 133	Cover over fasteners	
Figure 134	Different post supports	Ralph Bailey

WORKS CITED

A H Smith, H M Duggan, C Wright. 1994. "Assessment of cancer clusters using limited cohort data with spreadsheets: application to a leukaemia cluster among rubber workers." *Americal Journal of Industrial Medecine* 25 (6): 813-23.

American Wood Preservers Association. 2015. *Standard E12-94 Standard Method for Determining Corrosion of Metal in Contact with Treated Wood.* American Wood Preservers Association.

Arch Wood Protection, Inc. and Arch Treatment Technologies, Inc. 2006. *Hardware Recommendations for Treated Wood,.* Arch Wood Protection, Inc. and Arch Treatment Technologies, Inc.

Australian Government. n.d. *Unit of competencey details - AHCPGD305 - Conduct operational inspection of park facilities (Release 1).* Accessed January 27, 2021. https://training.gov.au/Training/Details/AHCPGD305.

—. n.d. *Unit of competency details - AHCPGD206 - Conduct visual inspection of park facilities (Release 1).* Accessed January 27, 2921. https://training.gov.au/Training/Details/AHCPGD206.

—. n.d. *Unit of competency details - AHCPGD505 - Conduct comprehensive inspection of park facilities (Release 1).* Accessed January 27, 2021. https://training.gov.au/Training/Details/AHCPGD505.

Australian Pesticides and Veterinary Medicines Authority. 2005. *The Reconsideration of Registrations of Arsenic Timber Treatment Products (CCA and arsenic trioxide) and Their Associated Labels - Report Of Review Findings And Regulatory Outcomes Final Report Part 1 - Toxicological Assessment.* Accessed December 7, 2020. https://apvma.gov.au/sites/default/files/publication/14316-arsenic-summary.pdf.

British Standards Institution. 1995. *Durability of wood and wood-based products. Natural durability of solid wood. Guide to natural durability and treatability of selected wood species of importance in Europe.* London: British Standards Institution.

Colin MacKenzie, C H Wang, R H Leicester, G C Foliente, M N Nguyen. 2020. *Timber service life design - Design guide for durability.* Melbourne: Wood Solutions.

Consulting Coordination Australia. 2020. *Enhance Advisory - 0720 - Playground Compliance.* Sydney: Consulting Coordination Australa.

—. 2018. *Enhance Advisory - 0917 - What Needs Certification (Play, Fitness, Parkour, Skate).* Version 3. Sydney: Consulting Coordination Australa.

—. 2018. *Ensuring Compliance of Equipment (Play, Fitnes, Parkour, Skate).* Version 3. Sydney: Consulting Coordination Australa.

—. 2018. *Timber Splitting and Cracking Rectification.* Version 1. Sydney: Consulting Coordination Australia.

Cookson, L.J. 2004. *The In-ground Natural Durability of Austyralian Timbers.* Melbourne: Forest and Wood Products Research and Development Corporation.

CSIRO. n.d. Accessed April 21, 2012. http://www.csiro.au/en/Outcomes/Food-and-Agriculture/CCATreatedTimber/CCA-safety-overview.aspx.

Department of Agriculture and Fisheries. 2020. *Construction Timbers in Queensland Book 1: Definitions and*

Descriptions. Brisbane: Queensland Government.

—. 2020. *Construction Timbers in Queensland Book 2: Properties and Specifications.* Brisbane: Queensland Government.

Dulux. n.d. *Weathershield Gloss Datasheet.* Accessed January 31, 2021. http://www.duspec.com.au/duspec/file/AUDD0054.pdf.

Dunisch, Oliver, Hans-Georg Richter, Gerald Koc. 2010. "Wood properties of juvenile and mature heartwood in Robinia pseudoacacia L." *Wood Science and Technology Journal* 44: 301-313.

Energex. 2020. *Manual 00302 Overhead Design Manual.* Brisbane: Energex.

Evans, Philip D. 2016. "The Effect of Incising on the checking of wood; A review." *International Wood Products Journal* 7 (1): 12-25.

Evans, Philip D., Jonathan G. Haase, A. Shakri, B.M. Seman and Makoto Kiguchi. 2015. "The Search for Durable Exterior Clear Coatings for Wood." *Coatings* 830-864.

Evans, Philip D., Robin Wingate-Hill, Simon C. Barry. 2000. "The Effects of Different Kerfing and Centre-boring Treatments on the Checking of ACQ Treated Pine Posts Exposed to the Weather." *Forest Products Journal* 50 (2): 59-64.

Forest and Wood Products Australia. 2007. *Manual 6 – Embedded corrosion of fasteners in exposed timber structures.* Melbourne: Forest and Wood products Australia.

Forpark. n.d. *Essentials.* Accessed March 6, 2021. https://www.forparkaust.com.au/wp-content/uploads/2019/09/Essentials-Material-Specifications-2019.pdf.

Gaslvanisers Association of Australia. U.D. *Hot Dipped Galvanising - The best protection inside and out.* Melbourne: Gaslvanisers Association of Australia.

Gaslvanisers Association of Queensland. U.D. *Atmospheric Corrosion Resistance of Hot Dipped Galvanized Coatings.* Melbourbe: Gaslvanisers Association of Queensland.

Huber, Rolf. 2020. *Health Effects of Tyre Rubber Exposure.* 7 December. https://playgroundprofessionals.com/surfaces/rubber/health-effects-tire-rubber-exposure.

John Lysaght. 1985. *The Lysaght Referee.* 27. Sydney: John Lysaght.

Kidsafe Victoria. n.d. *Actions to Reduce Playground Injuries.* Accessed May 28, 2012. http://www.kidsafevic.com.au/news/25-action-to-reduce-playground-injuries.

Lanotec . n.d. *Timber Seal Safety Data Sheet.* Accessed January 31, 2021. https://www.lanotec.com.au/wp-content/uploads/SDS-Timber-Seal-Sep-2017.pdf.

Li, Z.W., N.J. Marston and M.S. Jones. 2011. *Corrosion of Fasteners in Treated Timber Study Report SR241.* Branz.

One Steel Trading. No publication details. *DuraGal Flooring System – Issue 6.* One steel trading.

Orrcon Steel. No publication details. *Datasheet - ALLGAL Sept 2020 Rev 03.* Orrcon Steel.

Proludic S.A,S. n.d. *Origin by proludic, Play value naturally.* Vignon: Proludic.

Pryda Australia. 2014. *Technical Update, Corrosion Resistance of Pryda Products.* Dandenong south: Pryda Australia.

Queensland Government. n.d. *QTimber.* Accessed December 29, 2020. https://qtimber.daf.qld.gov.au.

Rammer, Douglas, Samuel Zelinka, Philip Line. 2006. "Fastener Corrosion: Testing, Research and Design Considerations ." *9th World Conference on Timber Engineering.* Portland. Pages not numbered.

Read, Deborah. n.d. *Report on Copper Chrome Arsenic Treated Timber.* Accessed February 14, 2021. https://www.epa.govt.nz/assets/Uploads/Documents/Hazardous-Substances/Guidance/Report-on-CCA-safety-by-Deborah-Read-April-2003.pdf.

Richter Spielgerate GmbH. No Publication Details. *Splits (Shakes) in Timber.* Richter Spielgerate GmbH.

Sentinel Group. n.d. *Fastener Safety Levels and Why They're Vital to Public Safety.* Accessed February 10, 2021. https://blog.sentinelgrp.com.au/fastener-security-levels-and-why-theyre-vital-to-public-safety/.

Simpson Strong-Tie. 2008. *Preservative Treated Wood Technical Bulletin No. T-PRWOOD08-R.* Pleasanton: Simpson Strong-Tie.

Standards Australia. 2019. *AS 4685.0 -2017 Amd 1:2019 Playground equipment and surfacing, Part 0: Development, installation, inspection, maintenance and operation.* Sydney: Stadards Australia.

—. 2021. *AS 4685.1:2021 Playground equipment and surfacing, Part 1: General safety requirements and test methods.* Sydney: Stabdards Australia.

—. 2012. *AS1604.1-2012 Specification for preservative treatment Sawn and round timber.* Sydney: Standards Australia.

—. 2010. *AS1720.1 – 2010 Timber structures, Part 1: Design methods.* Sydney: Standards Australia.

—. 1999. *AS2796.1-1999 Timber—Hardwood—Sawn and milled products, Part 1: product description.* Sydney: Standards Australia.

—. 1999. *AS2796.1-1999 Timber—Hardwood—Sawn and milled products, Part 2: Grade description.* Sydney: Standards Australia.

—. 2009. *AS3818.11-2009 Timber-heavy structural products-Visually graded, Part 11: Utility Poles.* Sydney: Standards Australia.

—. 2014. *AS4685.1-2014 Playground equipment and surfacing, Part 1: General safety requirements and test methods.* Sydney: Standards Australia.

—. 2005. *AS5604-2005 Timber – Natural durability ratings .* Sydney: Standards Australia.

n.d. *Stay Safe Around Copper Chrome Arsenate Treated Wood.* Accessed December 7, 2020. ttps://healthywa.wa.gov.au/Articles/S_T/Stay-safe-around-copper-chrome-arsenate-treated-wood.

Stirling, Rod. 2009. "Natural Durability Classification Systems Used Around the World." *IRG40.* Bejing: The International Research Group on Wood Protection.

Stubbersfield, Edgar. 2014. *The Seven Deadly Sins of External Timber Design - Revised.* Gatton: Rachel Stubbersfield.

Symbio Alliance. n.d. *Analysis of sealing CCA treated timber with Tanacoat.* Accessed February 11, 2021. https://www.outdoorstructures.com.au/pdf/cca_timber_treatment_analysis.pdf.

—. n.d. *Methodology of testing CCA treated timber.* Accessed February 11, 2021. https://www.outdoorstructures.com.au/pdf/cca_timber_treatment_methodology.pdf.

Taubmans. n.d. *Sunproof.* Accessed January 31, 2021. http://www.taubmans.com.au/Paints/Sun-Proof.

The Road and Traffic Authority. 2011. *Timber truss road bridges - A strategic approach to conservation.* Sydney: New South Wales Government.

The Wood Database. n.d. *Black Locust.* Accessed January 26, 2018. http://www.wood-database.com/black-locust/.

Timber Queensland. 2014. *Technical data Sheet 20, Residential Timber Fences.* Brisbane: Timber Queensland.

—. 2014. *Technical Data Sheet No. 9 Timber Retaining Walls for Residential Applications.* Brisbane: Timber Queensland.

Timber Secretarial Group. U.D. *Dictionary of Timber Terms.* Sydney: Timber Secretarial Group.

TTT Products. n.d. *Unilog.* Accessed December 28, 2020. https://www.unilog.co.nz/product-7-unilog.

Wattyl. n.d. *Solarguard Ultra Premium Low Sheen Data Sheet.* Accessed January 31, 2021. http://services.valsparprofessional.com.au/uploads/tds/D4.14%20-%20Solagard%20Low%20Sheen.pdf.

2010. *Wood in Australia, Types, Properties and Uses.* 2. Sydney: McGraw-Hill Education.

Wood Solutions. n.d. *Visual Stress Grading.* Accessed October 19, 2020. https://www.woodsolutions.com.au/articles/visual-stress-grading Date.

Wvans, Philip D., Robin Wingate-Hill, Simon C. Barry. 1997. "The Ability of Physical Treatments to Reduce Checking in Preservative-treated Slash Pine Posts." *Australian Forest Journal* 47 (5): 51-55.

Zelinka, Samuel L. 2014. "Corrosion of Metals in Wood Products." In *Developments in Corrosion Potection*, by Mahmood Aliofkhazraei, 568-592. InTech.

ABOUT THE AUTHORS

Edgar (Ted) Stubbersfield is a third generation sawmiller who has become arguably Australia's foremost authority on how to detail weather exposed timber. His products were regarded as industry leading in the way they outlasted and outperformed those of his competitors. He is a prolific author specialising in different aspects of weather exposed timber use

Ralph Bailey is an AIA Life Fellow and was the joint founder of the multi-award-winning architectural practice Guyer Bailey Architects with Tim Guymer. With a passion for creating play areas that enliven all of the senses and create suitable physical challenges, Ralph has designed some of Queensland's most highly regarded playgrounds, such as Frew Park Arena in Brisbane and Kings Beach in Caloundra, that help people unlock their imaginations, learn to manage risk and get back to nature. Ralph has had an impressive career spanning five decades that also includes teaching at QUT for 17 years, publishing several papers and books on design and landscaping, and being a pioneer in eco-tourism with Tim Guymer on the Kingfisher Bay Resort project. Ralph's experience and knowledge of Australian timbers especially hardwoods led to his cooperation with Ted Stubbersfield to produce this book titled "Timber in Playgrounds" to seek to correct some of the problems that have occurred and are still occurring in timber playgrounds.

www.ingramcontent.com/pod-product-compliance
Lightning Source LLC
Chambersburg PA
CBHW060812010526
44117CB00002B/17